KU-058-466

Tangerman's
Basic Whittling
and Woodcarving

E.J. Tangerman

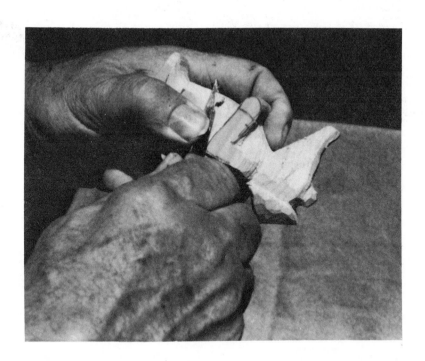

Sterling Publishing Co., Inc. New York
Distributed in the U.K. by Blandford Press

Other books by E. J. Tangerman

Capturing Personality in Woodcarving
Carving Faces and Figures in Wood
Carving Flora and Fables in Wood
Carving Religious Motifs in Wood
Carving Wooden Animals
Carving the Unusual

Library of Congress Cataloging in Publication Data

Tangerman, E. J. (Elmer John), 1907–
  Tangerman's Basic whittling and woodcarving.

  (Home craftsman series)
  Includes index.
  1. Wood-carving. I. Title. II. Title: Basic
whittling and woodcarving. III. Series.
TT199.7.T328 1983   731.4′62   83-4847
ISBN 0-8069-7778-7

Edited by Michael Cea

Copyright © 1983 by Sterling Publishing Co., Inc.
Two Park Avenue, New York, N.Y. 10016
Distributed in Australia by Oak Tree Press Co., Ltd.
P.O. Box K514 Haymarket, Sydney 2000, N.S.W.
Distributed in the United Kingdom by Blandford Press
Link House, West Street, Poole, Dorset BH15 1LL, England
Distributed in Canada by Oak Tree Press Ltd.
% Canadian Manda Group, P.O. Box 920, Station U
Toronto, Ontario, Canada M8Z 5P9
Manufactured in the United States of America

Contents

Fig. 1. Ancestral figure from the Sepik River, Papua New Guinea, dwarfs Mrs. Tangerman. It is carved from a single log and painted with lime, earth colors and charcoal from burned coconut shells.

Preface

How to carve more than shavings

When my son was learning to whittle, he would say, "Now I'm going to make a dog." After he had cut off a leg or two, he would settle for a fish, but the final admission would be, "I guess it's going to be another knife!" "Knife" was a euphemism for the pointed stick that country-store whittlers are always shown making. Wade Martin (see Chapter 8), when complimented on the latest of his excellent country carvings, would say shyly, "I'd ruther be whittlin' *somethin'* than just be whittlin' whittlins!"

There should and can be more than just shavings for an end product in carving. What's more, the end product should vary; constant output of the same thing is too much like Detroit and automobiles. That is why I have spent as much time as I could spare this past half century hunting up new designs to carve. In recent years, many of these have been from faraway places, because the nearby ones are described in my own and other books. I am still amazed at how good and free many primitive designs are, and how well they are executed, usually without the tools and equipment we consider necessary. You do not need a fancy shop to be a good woodcarver—which is one of its attractions for me.

This book includes more extensive summaries of basic information on tools and sharpening than I have written recently. It has some simple, but different, projects for beginning whittlers and carvers, then some more advanced ones, first for whittling with the knife alone, then for carving with a variety of tools. I have added appendices on sharpening, finishing and changing drawing size. The chapters on knives and chisels are as up-to-date and complete as I can make them. Wood selection and finishing are included piece by piece, but there is also a complete chapter on wood and its characteristics. All in all, I have tried to provide here a mini-handbook for experienced as well as beginning carvers. May your tools stay sharp and your wood and your ideas be unchecked!

E. J. Tangerman

CHAPTER I

Woods—Which and Where

Try what you have when you can—it may surprise you

When early man developed his first crude cutting edges he found wood to be an amenable and plentiful material and soon discovered differences in the characteristics of the various species available. There was so much work involved in his shaping of increasingly sophisticated things—whether they were tools, idols or toys—that he *had* to learn which wood was good and which was not, depending upon the final purpose of the piece.

In rural and remote areas this is still true to an extent, although in general we buy lumber from far away for local structures and usage and although the relative importance of wood as a material has been greatly reduced. Thus, the typical modern whittler or woodcarver must in most cases use what is readily available, whether or not it is ideal for his purposes. In other words, most of us carve lumber rather than trees and are limited to woods that are commercial locally. Furthermore, even in remote areas, a perfectly suitable local wood may be discarded in favor of something that must be bought even sight unseen from a catalogue; the resulting work is, therefore, limited by the particular block bought.

One example that leaps to mind is "mahogany," a word used to describe an increasingly divergent group of imported and expensive woods. There are mahoganies from Africa, Mexico, Cuba, Central and South America, and the Philippines. I have six samples from the Philippines, all presumably mahogany, that vary from almost white to a darkish red-brown, with the heaviest twice the weight of the lightest. And none of these is lauan or lauanda, now the usual surface veneer of "mahogany" plywood, or prima-vera, a white wood which when stained looks like good mahogany. The best mahogany is still that from Honduras, which is fine-grained although rela-tively soft. Cuban mahogany is dense and varies in hardness; South American varieties tend to be grainy and splinter easily; Philippine commonly available is coarse and the poorest of the lot.

So much for mahogany, which is so familiar because of its long record of use as a furniture wood. The best whittling wood is probably basswood, followed fairly closely by American white pine and imported Indonesian jelutong. These tend to be straight-grained and have few knots or other areas of difficulty. Carvings made from them will have little distinction in most cases unless tinted with stains, acrylic or oil paints, although the common tendency to stain them a standard color or paint them with solid colors is unfortunate. Of the so-called white pines, ponderosa is good if you avoid the strongly colored pieces. Sugar pine is a bit more porous. Avoid yellow pine, which is hard, often knotty, and resinous.

Among other soft woods are poplar, which bruises easily and tends to grip tools, so is hard to cut smoothly; cedar, which is also easy to cut but bruises and has a distinctive color; willow, which has a tendency to split; cypress, which does not wear well; and alder, a West Coast favorite usually carved green because the carving is easier and the wood does not check as it dries, at least in small pieces.

Many whittlers have always used local woods, particularly the fruit and nut woods. All are harder than those previously mentioned, tend to check and are subject to insect attack and warpage, but they will support more detail and undercutting, take a better finish and have a grain that does not interfere with carving and a color that makes painting unnecessary. Among them are pear, pecan, cherry, apple and black walnut. Cherry and black walnut are particularly good, the latter probably being the best American carving wood. It has a fine, tough grain and good color and finishes beautifully, but may turn quite dark if oiled. (This may be as much of a disadvantage as the whiteness of basswood or holly.)

There are many woods used for carving in the areas where they grow, like buckeye, cypress, cottonwood, poplar (gum), chestnut, willow, birch, maple, butternut and myrtle. Maple is much harder than the others, but takes a good finish and supports detail. Look out for warping and splitting with chestnut. Hickory, sycamore, beech and magnolia are hard to cut and good primarily for shallow carving. Ash is stringy but can be carved quite success-fully. Red oak is softer, darker and has a greater tendency to splinter than white; both are very hard. In the Southwest, there are available mesquite, ironwood and Osage orange, all slow-growing, dense and quite hard. They also are prone to splitting, but take a very good finish. You may know or have heard of others; the best advice I can give is to try them. I have carved macadamia from Hawaii, kerosene, garamut and kwila from the Trobriands.

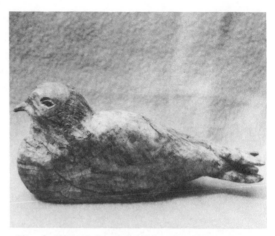

Fig. 3. Wood that is bad for the cabinetmaker may be good for the carver. This piece of spalted (partially dry-rotted) curly broadleaf maple makes a very intriguing stylized nighthawk that is 2½ × 4 × 9 in (6.4 × 10.2 × 22.9 cm).

Fig. 2. Black walnut, the best American carving wood, will support a great deal of detail but tends to be dark, as this snapshot of a coat of arms I recently carved shows. It is about 10 × 12 in (25.4 × 30.5 cm).

Fig. 4. Cedar tends to crush unless tools are very sharp, but this panel was worth the effort. The panel itself is a 1 × 5½ × 10-in (2.5 × 14 × 25.4-cm) piece of Western red cedar, from a log blasted to a dark grey in the Mount St. Helens eruption in 1981. Inlaid are three pieces of Virginia cedar, natural in color but 8,500 years old, plus or minus 500 years, according to a carbon-14 test. About the third oldest piece of wood known, the tree was found in a marl pit in Ohio several years ago.

Many woods are now imported in lumber that will cut into carving-size blocks or panels. They tend, however, to be relatively expensive, particularly in recent years. Among them, my favorite is teak from Thailand or Burma, which will support detail, does not warp appreciably, and is impervious to water, rot and insect attack. (Teak also comes from China and other sources, but this is harsh-grained.) It can be carved easily with chisels and mallet, but does often contain silica, which takes the edge off tools despite the deceptive smoothness of cutting created by the oil in the wood. This is true also of some kinds of rosewood, which like mahogany can come from many sources and vary widely in color and characteristics. I have pieces ranging from red to dark reddish-brown and even containing purple, green and yellow.

Fig. 5. This pillar from Bali was exhibited at the New York World's Fair in 1939. It is teak, with the carving of Siva on top made of blinding wood (also called blind-my-eyes in Australia because of its poisonous tendencies).

Lime and boxwood, both used extensively in Europe (and boxwood in China), are not readily available here. Both are hard and good cutting wood. European linden is like our basswood. English sycamore (called harewood when cut and stained in a particular way) carves well, and is white like our holly and available in wider boards. There are also available such woods as

English and Austrian oak, both more dense and finer-grained than our oaks, hence much used in religious carving. English walnut has too much "figure" for good carving usually; Italian walnut has a fine texture, close grain and cuts like English oak. Others surface occasionally, but Europe has fewer woods than we do, particularly if the 2,800 varieties growing in Mexico are included.

Many woods have been imported from Africa in recent years, mostly for veneers or specialty uses like pool cues and arrows. Others have been imported from Central and South America, so there are such woods as purpleheart, greenheart, bubinga, ambuya, beefwood, thuya, vermilion (amboina) and avodire, among many others. All are expensive, hard to find and finance in suitably sized pieces, and tend to be more trouble than they are worth unless you are after a special color, graining or other effect. I have carved most of them in making up fish and dinosaur mobiles each with 16 or more units of a different wood, but have found they tend to split and splinter, among other things. Lacewood, satinwood and sandalwood are scarce nowadays, but can be useful. There are also such woods as zebrawood, beautiful in grain but as hard to carve as American redwood or cypress because of variation in hardness between winter and summer wood.

Fig. 6. Grinling Gibbons was the most famous of English carvers and the great worker in lime. His floral swags have been popular for 400 years.

Fig. 7. One of the distinctive African woods is vermilion or amboina. It is a brilliant dark red in color. I carved this panel, about 12 × 19 in (30.5 × 48.3 cm), in vermilion to go outside a door on a modern brown-stained house. The wood is spectacular when finished, but tends to splinter when carved to such detail as this.

Popular among sculptors are such woods as ebony, cocobolo, and lignum vitae, all very hard but capable of fine finishing. (The latter two are called "ironwood" locally in Mexico because they sink in water, and may also be called guayacan.) Ebony is really another general term, because the wood comes from Africa, India, Indonesia (particularly the Celebes—now Sulawesi), Ceylon (now Sri Lanka) and South and Central America. It varies in color and marking from solid black (Gabon and New Guinea) to dark brown with black striping (macassar from Sulawesi and calamander from Sri Lanka), and black with lighter striping (striped or swirled ebony from New Guinea). All these woods, as well as rosewood and mahogany, can create lung-inflammatory dust when sanded

I should mention pink ivorywood from Africa which is the world's most expensive wood, something like $300 a pound at this writing. It has been described, apocryphally, I think, as the private wood of the Zulu kings; anyone else found with it was beheaded. It varies from pinkish white to dark pink, is relatively hard and tends to split, and in my opinion is more a curiosity than a useful carving wood. I have a couple of pieces and use it on occasion for jewelry.

11

If you have a particular interest in identifying various species, beware of such countries as Mexico. One day in Oaxaca, I visited half a dozen one-man carpenter shops within blocks of each other. In several I found exotic woods and got samples with their local names written on. Each carpenter had a different name for the same wood, and there is no publication that begins to identify them. There are good guide books in the United States, as well as the International Wood Collectors Society (current secretary-treasurer, Bruce T. Forness, IWCS, Drawer B, Main St., Chaumont, N.Y. 13622) that publishes a monthly *Bulletin* containing much information on available woods. Considering, however, that there are something like 7,000 species of wood in the world, identifying the odd foreign piece is almost hopeless. As I said initially, try carving it, and good luck!

Fig. 8 (left). Real ebony is becoming very scarce because it is being carved up much faster than it can grow. Bali, for example, must import it from a rapidly diminishing supply in the Celebes (Sulawesi), largely because so much was used on carvings like this one, about four feet (1.2 m) tall —and sold to tourists for a song some years back. Fig. 9 (above). These two lengths of Mexican "blanco" about 2 in (5.1 cm) in diameter, I carved in the images of the old Aztec gods. It is very much like white pine.

CHAPTER II
Start with a Good Knife

Whittling requires a first-class tool

The original Old English usage of the word "whittling," which referred to a butcher knife, is now largely obsolete. The word whittling is still very much in use in the United States, however. American dictionaries define it as meaning "to cut or shape a piece of wood by slowly paring it away with a knife." The word is also used by reputable historical groups to apply to paring operations with *any* single tool like a drawknife, spokeshave, or adz for such winter farm operations as making handles for tools, wagon and harness parts—in fact, wherever a single tool predominates and makes many small paring cuts.

I defined whittling a half century ago as meaning "carving with a clasp knife a one-piece object of wood, usually small enough to be held in the hand." In recent years, however, there has been an increasing tendency to loosen the definition, so the "whittling" category at shows can include anything (particularly chains, fans, balls-in-a-cage and similar "tricks") regardless of size in which the principal tool is the knife (or several different shapes of a knife), even though sandpaper—a means of cutting chips—has been liberally used and small chisels applied for complex cuts. This is incorrect, but Americans tend to broaden definitions to suit their convenience. I shall try, however, to be as precise as possible!

A good knife is of course the first essential for whittling. There was a time when selection was not difficult; most hardware dealers carried good-quality pocketknives at reasonable prices, and someone could offer sound advice on which knife to select for a particular purpose. Nowadays, knives tend to be flimsy and decorative rather than sturdy and reliable, with metal bodies and poor-quality stainless-steel blades. Furthermore, the seller probably has never whittled, so his advice is meaningless.

What's more, many whittlers are former toolmakers or other skilled craftsmen and cannot resist the temptation to apply some ingenuity to redesign; as a consequence, there is an endless variety in knife and handle shapes in craft shops and advertised in crafts magazines. These range from special handle or blade shapes or materials to mechanical wonders that hold almost as many blades as a Swiss Army knife. In recent years, one of the most common specialties has been a screw-chuck handle and a series of blades of various shapes like concave-edged ones, right- and left-handed hook blades for hollowing cavities, and even small chisels. Some have handles of exotic woods, or handles that the buyer can shape to suit his grip, his fancy, and so on. We have as well the knives the whittler makes himself, from anything that has some temper, ranging from old springs, straight razors, jointer blades, discarded or broken saw blades to ice picks. Many of the better ones become collector's items.

Basically, however, no one has ever surpassed the old-fashioned pocketknife as an all-around versatile tool. It is compact, convenient and sturdy; a two- or three-bladed jackknife and a two-bladed smaller pocketknife constitute a first-class portable woodcarving shop. These knives have carbon-steel blades that will rust from perspiration, but which also hold an edge better than stainless-steel blades. The handles are usually wood or horn and comfortable to grip. The blades can snap shut on an unwary finger if they are mishandled, but they also offer no hazard when not in use because the edge is covered; any special knife with a fixed blade must be equipped with a sheath if carried at all, and it is longer-handled and heavier. Knives with chuck handles or lock-in interchangeable blades appear to be more versatile, but interchanging the blades and finding a storage place for the extras can be a nuisance. Also, chucks have a nasty habit of allowing the blade to rotate unexpectedly under pressure. Some popular makes have blades too thin to stand real cutting force, or too soft for cutting hard woods.

My opinions are, I admit, somewhat biased because I grew up using pocketknives as major tools, and after 75 years I still fall back on the pocketknife when the going gets rough. I carry two pocketknives—one a jackknife with three blades, the other a penknife with two. I have tried sloyd knives, barrel knives and lock-blade knives and have found them a nuisance or too heavy. At home I often use a special knife with a blade shape I like, plus two heavy-duty interchangeable-blade knives of the chuck type, one with a thick and stubby, but pointed, blade, the other with a concave-edged blade of the kind designed originally for leather cutting. They are easier on my aging hands and I can interchange blades when one gets dull without undue time loss.

When the chips are down (or *not down* in whittling), however, I find myself reaching for my pocketknife. It gets into places no other tool will, and gets me out of trouble that other tools create. A pocket slip or stone takes care of touch-ups on blade edges if necessary, but a good knife will hold an edge for anything from an hour to half a day of steady whittling. (At home, the small stone can be supplemented with fine-grit ones and a single or double strop, of course.)

If you are starting to whittle, and intend to make hand-size items in soft wood, use a first-class pocketknife with carbon-steel blades, one pen and one B-clip (see Fig. 10, page 16). A third blade can be a spear, a cutoff pen or a sheepfoot. The straight-cutting edge of the latter shapes has some advantages in rounding convex surfaces and attaining flatness, but tends to drag at the heel in any hollow cutting. No blade should be longer than about 1½ in (3.81 cm). Be sure the pivots are tight and the springs strong, so the blade opens and stays open, without wobbling. Beware of excrescences like cork-screws and clevises (for belt hooks); they will cause sore palms and blisters.

As you progress, add fixed-blade knives for protracted use—avoid the straight blade and rounded tip of some such knives. Or add a chuck handle with several shapes of blades, but be certain the handle fits your hand well and the chuck can be screwed up tightly on sturdy blades. The thin blades are useful only for extremely delicate work.

Contrary to the old Boy Scout adage that you must always cut away from yourself, the whittler must be able to cut in any direction, as indicated on pages 16 and 17; his best cut, in fact, is one resembling potato peeling in that the force is put behind the blade simply by clenching the hand. Particularly on soft wood, the knife must be kept very sharp, so no real force is necessary to cut, because heavy arm-muscle force is hard to control and causes accidents.

Be conscious all the time that the knife has a fairly long cutting edge, and never get anything in front of that edge unless you intend to cut it. This is meant particularly to apply to the hand holding the work and to the cutting-hand thumb on paring cuts. Many beginning whittlers protect their thumbs with fingerstalls of rubber, sold by stationery shops for sorting papers. The skilled whittler does not need such things—he rarely cuts himself. (I do only when demonstrating or being otherwise inattentive.) You can't whittle and talk or watch television.

Beware of sticking the blade tip into the wood and exerting pressure; the

Fig. 10. Knife cuts using two hands.

LEFT INDEX-FINGER ASSIST
Shaving cuts. Work must be clamped or held by left hand

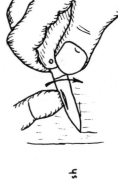

LEFT-INDEX DRAW CUT
Shaving + detailing. Gives close control with more force

GUILLOTINE CUT
Adds force at blade tip.
Left index finger or thumb push

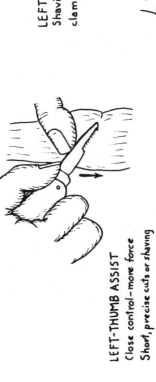

LEFT-THUMB ASSIST
Close control – more force
Short, precise cuts or shaving

Pen   Spear   Spey   B-Clip   Sheepfoot   Crescent or Hook   Cut-off   Pen   Carver's   Chip

Fig. 11. Knife blade shapes.

16

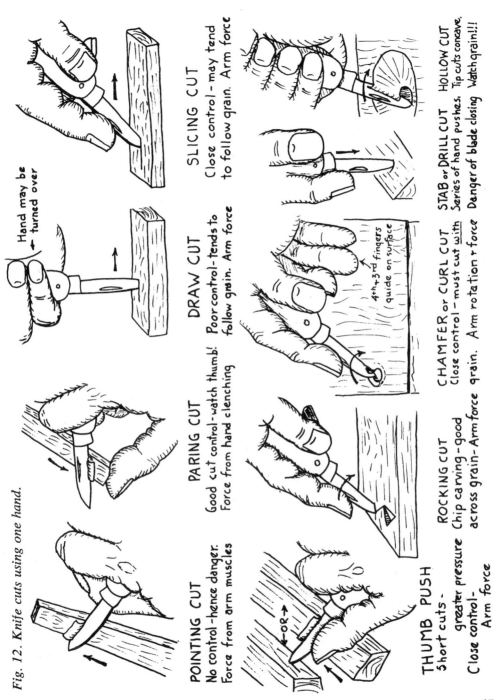

Fig. 12. Knife cuts using one hand.

Hand may be turned over

SLICING CUT
Close control – may tend to follow grain. Arm force

HOLLOW CUT
Tip cuts concave. Watch grain!!

DRAW CUT
Poor control – tends to follow grain. Arm force

STAB or DRILL CUT
Series of hand pushes. Danger of blade closing

PARING CUT
Good cut control – watch thumb! Force from hand clenching

4th + 3rd fingers guide on surface

CHAMFER or CURL CUT
Close control – must cut with grain. Arm rotation r force

POINTING CUT
No control – hence danger. Force from arm muscles

ROCKING CUT
Chip carving – good across grain – Arm force

THUMB PUSH
Short cuts – greater pressure Close control – Arm force

– or –

17

blade may close on your fingers. For the same reason, always hold the body of the knife in your fingertips when closing a blade, and make the final closure with the palm of your hand. Never have two blades open at once. On a folding blade, there is a boss that prevents a finger from slipping onto the cutting edge; many of the special knives are not thus protected.

It is obvious that a blade should not be hammered, or used for miscellaneous cutting, like paper or fingernails, or for skinning electric wire. Also, it should not be sharpened on a wheel unless it is nicked or chipped; then it should be cooled twice as often as you consider necessary. Cutting newly sanded areas or scraping a surface takes off a newly honed edge faster than a half day of cutting. Occasional oiling of both blade and pivots will help to retard rusting, particularly in summer.

When the knife is used, chip size should be adjusted to the wood and the design. It is a delight to cut big chips in soft wood, but they tend to be hard to control, so you may cut beyond your intended lines or generate a split. It is advisable to make a stop cut *across* the grain before you attempt to make a cut to that point *with* the grain. The harder the wood or the greater its tendency to split, the smaller the chips should be. Also, chip size should be reduced as you approach finishing dimensions.

Rough all areas before any one is finished; this way a gash or nick can still be corrected. Chips should be cut out, not wedged out; wedging may break the blade tip and will certainly bruise or dent the wood fibres against which the knife is pressed.

In cutting a slot or a V-groove, it is advisable to make the end stop cuts first, then cut down the center with the knife tip, before cutting the two sides in towards the center. This gives better control of groove shape. It is important to cut *with* the grain whenever possible because any angling cut will be clean on the side *running out* of the grain, but tends to tear and run in on the side *entering* the grain. Thus, grain should always be considered when laying out a design and when its outlines are being carved. (In some woods, cuts with the grain in one direction may cause trouble which can be avoided by reversing the cutting direction.)

When possible, cuts across-grain should be made first. Across-grain cuts take more force than those with the grain, so there is increased chance of error. Also, when across-grain cuts and with-grain cuts are alternated, the difference in force required and the fact that an across-grain chip tends to crumble must always be kept in mind. The "hollow cut" in Fig. 12 provides a good example of this.

When the blade enters the grain, it tends to tear and split the wood ahead of it, while on the exiting portions it cuts smoothly; thus a conical cut like that illustrated in Fig. 12 is best made with four quarter cuts, each with the grain, rather than one continuous one. A pointed blade can be used directly as a drill by simply rotating it, but the same danger of tearing exists in that case. In general, when it is necessary to whittle across the grain or around knots or other likely grain variations, it is advisable to make very light cuts and observe the action of the blade constantly to determine when cutting direction should be changed. (In this kind of situation, the woodcarver reaches for a riffler file.)

If you keep your knife sharp and cut accurately and cleanly, sanding should not be necessary. With occasional exceptions, a whittled piece is the better for having the slight planes left by the knife; they catch the light and show that the piece is not formed plastic. Further, sanding tends to smear the surface, and, particularly on harder woods, will dull the clean gloss surface left by the tool. If you must sand, use worn fine sandpaper sparingly.

Fig. 13. This ¾ × 9¼ × 16-in (1.9 × 23.5 × 40.6-cm) teak panel includes 119 separate designs, including 50 common flowers of the Eastern seaboard and the leaves of 42 trees and bushes plus a dozen of their flowers and fruits. Hidden among them is a personal history of my good friend Fred Ritter. Visible are the tower of the Cornell library (his college), a sailing dinghy, part of a piano keyboard, a trumpet, a tennis racket, six bust portraits showing lead theatrical roles he played in amateur theatre, a pair of choristers, Alice (his wife's name) from Tenniel's "Alice in Wonderland," as well as the New York (sugar maple) and Georgia (live oak) state trees, the Georgia state flower (dogwood) and the violet, his fraternity flower.

CHAPTER III
Whittle Gnomes

Caricatures show step-by-step use of the knife

These three Oriental gnomes are adapted from a little figure I saw in Tokyo as a decoration in a jeweler's showcase. They are caricatures, of course, and quite simple in shape as well as adaptable to a number of poses. All can be pine or basswood, and painted. The seated and bent-over figures are each 3¼ in (8.3 cm) long, the nose-in-the-air one just under 4 in (10.2 cm) tall. The blanks are sawed out of 1-in (2.5-cm) wood, and will also serve here to amplify the instructions on handling the knife in the previous chapter. The procedure is shown in Figs. 16–21.

GROUND WATCHER
MUSICIAN→

SKY WATCHER
ORIENTAL GNOMES
White pine-painted

Fig. 14.

Fig. 15 (above). Oriental gnomes whittled from 1-in (2.5-cm) white pine and painted with oils. Grains run with the beard in each case. All are caricatures, with stylized bulbous noses, slanted eyes and no mouths or ears. Fig. 16 (below left). After the blanks are sawed, they are roughed to shape. Point the hat and beard by paring cuts where possible, and thumb-push cuts otherwise. The arms and coat bottom are then shaped. Fig. 17 (below right). Make outline or stop cuts across grain first. Here the knife is being drawn along the line of the bottom of the arm of the seated figure, so slices can be cut from the skirt of the coat up to them. This cut is made by pressing the edge in as it is drawn along the line.

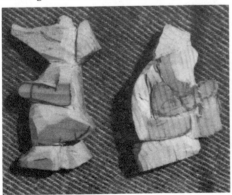

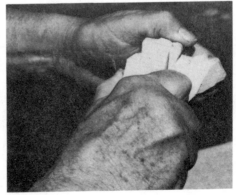

21

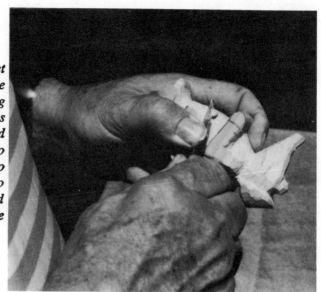

Fig. 18. Some cuts are best made by pushing the knife edge, rather than paring with it. However, push cuts are made with the arm and are difficult to control. So the left hand, in addition to holding the blank, is used to provide easily controlled thumb force behind the blade.

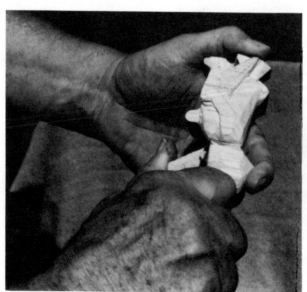

Fig. 19. The paring cut, like that used in peeling a potato, is the most generally useful and easiest to control of cutting srokes. It is advisable, however, to wear a thumb stall to protect the ball of the thumb until you have considerable experience.

Fig. 20. Grain runs with the beard on each figure. The stooping figure is completed, but details of the right arm and umbrella on the other figure have been sketched but not cut. The central "lump" on the chest is for the left hand, so wood must be cut away from the chest by rocking the blade as it is drawn along the line of the chest, then wafer cuts can be made from each side to clear away waste.

Fig. 21. The procedure of cutting the arm free is shown on the seated figure, while on the standing one the arm, umbrella and coat bottom have been outlined, waste wood cut away, and the shapes modelled with a short blade. If outlining is done thoroughly and cleanly, the modelling of the arm, umbrella and nose is rapid. The eyes are formed by cutting slits with the knife; pupils will be painted black spots.

CHAPTER IV
Whittle Small Silhouettes

Neckerchief slides, bolos, pins and pendants are easy and fast

Probably the most popular whittling project among Boy Scouts has been the neckerchief slide. The late Ben Hunt designed and described a number of them. H. M. Sutter of Portland, Oregon, designed a number as well, and sold blanks for them. The same designs can be used for pendants, pins and bolos, and many can be carved extensively or simply be painted silhouettes, depending upon the maker. The primary shape is provided by the silhouette itself, and modelling is minimal, so the designs are very practical for beginning whittlers.

I have sketched about 40 of Mr. Sutter's designs, and pictured others. They are basically silhouettes jigsawed from ¼- to ⅜-in (6.4- to 9.5-mm) pine or basswood, although they can be made of harder woods, and thicker if more modelling is desired, as on the Indian chief head or the thunderbird. Most of the designs are variants of a few basic shapes. Most versatile is the shield, which from a defensive weapon became the principal basis for heraldry. Family escutcheons or coats of arms can be carved on a shield background, but it can also be used as a blank for arrowheads, masks, and can be turned sidewise or upside down to provide a blank for animals, birds and fish. It can be rounded as a plain boss also.

The arrow is a popular slide design; it can be interpreted in a variety of ways, depending upon the skill of the individual. The hiker sole or shoe sole is similar in that the shape itself is simple. It can be whittled as a sole with a date and/or location. However, it can also be carved into several quite complex shapes, like the lobster, fish and duck. The same is true of the canoe paddle, which with a little interpretation becomes a snowshoe, fiddle or tennis racket.

The owl and covered wagon are just for fun; both are somewhat more complex. The thunderbird is one of the most used and most significant of Western Indian designs, often changed in detail to suit the whim of the maker. It is used on rugs, pins, baskets, beaded items, costumes and jewelry.

ARROW ¼ x ¾ x 2¾"
Head and feathering may be thinned, head and shaft shaped

Blank
Groove
Scallop
Hollow

V-groove
css
Chip-carved
CROSS ¼ x 1½ x 2⅛"

Blank
Paint
CANOE ¼ x ⅝ x 2½"
Round top & bottom, thin ends
¼ x 1½ x 2½"

ARROWHEAD
Scallop surface to suggest stone flaking

Blank ¼ x ¾ x 3"
Thin to ½
Incise design
Incise
CANOE PADDLE & THREE VARIANTS

Blank ¼ x 1¼ x 1½"

Sink ⅟₃
INTERLACINGS

Blank ¼ x ½ x 2⅝"
Our Camp '82
HIKER SOLE - ¼ x 1½ x 2¼"

Blank ¼ x 1⅛ x 2½"
Thin head   about ⅓
V-notch
Chip-   carved
Rounded
THUNDERBIRD
A favorite Indian design & widely varied

Blank ¼ x 1¼ x 1½"

SHIELD & VARIANTS - ¼ x 1⅛ x 2¼"

Blank
OWL - ¼ x 1½ x 3"

DOUBLE CARRICK BEND & SQUARE KNOT (Left) ¼ x 1½ x 2⅛"

¼ x 1½ x 2⅞"
COVERED WAGON

Fig. 22. Some typical bolo patterns.

Fig. 23. Some indication of the variety of neckerchief slides is given by these peg-boards, which show blanks and some of the carvings possible from them.

The square knot is the most useful knot, and so is very familiar in scouting and elsewhere. This is a more complex carving because it involves a good deal of precise modelling. Even more complicated is the double carrick bend, a more complex knot used for joining two hawsers. Similar in difficulty are the intertwined six-point star and the crossed links.

The problem on all of these designs is to use soft wood and carve it without splitting off sections with the grain. It is very easy, for example, to split off the feathering or points of the arrow or the ends of the canoe, the head of the thunderbird, or the arms of the cross, and easier still to break out sections that are chip-carved.

If made into neckerchief slides as Mr. Sutter did it, a second piece of wood with a ¾-in (19.1-mm) hole drilled in it is simply glued edgewise on the back. It is also possible, of course, to whittle the slide in a thicker block, so the hole is integral. The same designs can be used for bolos, although in this case it is necessary to have the "finding" to fasten on the back, or to make it. To make a pin, a "finding" with a flat-backed pin can be glued on, or one made by gluing a safety pin into a slot. In any case, the piece should be brightly painted unless it is in a fine wood.

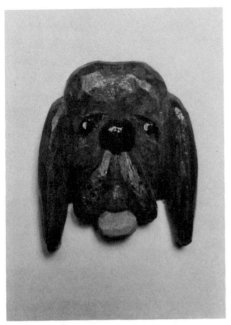

Figs. 24–27. These slides are all derived from the shield blank, but can, of course, be cut out directly to shape. Clockwise, they are: dog, pineapple, butterfly and eagle.

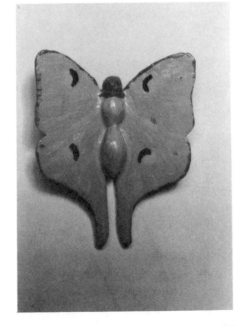

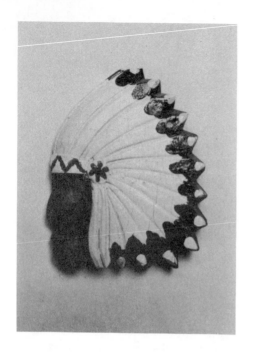 

Figs. 28–31. More examples of neckerchief slides. Clockwise, they are: Indian head-dress, bird, knot and wagon.

 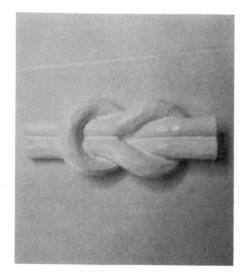

Fig. 32. Two versions of the cross are both chip-carved, and make excellent pendants.

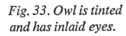Fig. 33. Owl is tinted
and has inlaid eyes.

CHAPTER V
Enjoy—as the Primitives Do!

Indians in Mexico, Peru and Argentina "do their thing"

After years of visiting primitive carvers in many countries, I am still surprised at the quality and originality of much of their work. Some of it is, of course, merely crude, but some is good caricature, some good realism, some good stylizing. Most of us have been exposed to "art"—good or bad—so we tend to be inhibited by what we have learned. This is not a problem for an Indian in Mexico or Peru, or a native in the South Pacific. They let themselves go, and carve what they really feel or see without too much concern for what other people think. They do, however, eventually become somewhat circumscribed by the necessity for eating, and tend to make more of what will sell; they cannot carve as a hobby, as so many of us do.

In any case, I have put together here some examples from various Latin American countries, mostly Mexico, of primitive carvings of animals. None is complicated, so they will provide good, and very different, exercises for a whittler. There are, for example, several skeletons, the outgrowth of the Latin American Day of the Dead, November 1, something like our Halloween, but with much more adult participation and religious overtones. I have had skeletons of men and animals in all sorts of poses, and carved from woods like copal and tsumpantli. I show some here because of the tremendous imagination their carvers exhibit.

Another interesting development is animals utilizing the natural shape of a branch, and/or with legs and ears nailed on! There are also, from the Patzcuaro area, whittled figures of the *Viejitos* (little old men), who do a very popular series of dances, actually so strenuous that young men, masked as old men, must do them. And mixed in are strange figures that seem to date back to an earlier time, or to a half-remembered legend.

The pictures will, in most instances, explain themselves. To make them, all you need is soft wood, a sharp knife and some imagination. And you can paint them in gaudy colors as the natives do!

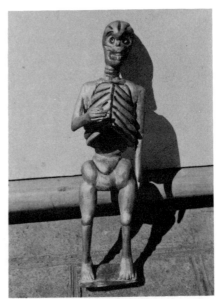

Fig. 34 (above). Standing human skeletons from Mexico, one 10 in (25.4 cm) tall in copal and unpainted (left), the other 2½ ft (76.2 cm) and colored (right). Note that the skeleton is modified for ease in carving. Fig. 35 (below). Ten-in (25.4-cm) trumpeter, fiddler and kneeling skeleton with a candle are all of copal and from San Martin, Tilcajete, Mexico. Bent arms are usually from bent branches, which are nailed on.

Fig. 36 (above left). Skeleton tower, about 10 in (25.4 cm) high, is primarily skulls, but has complete figures on two sides. Fig. 37 (above right). Four-eyed mermaid with harp, carved by Celestin Cruz of San Martin, is a pierced panel about 2 ft (61.0 cm) high, with eyes in the back of the head, skulls on shoulders, and a free-form instrument. Fig. 38 (below). Several poses of Los Viejitos, *from Patzcuaro, including one frowning and one with cloth additions.*

Fig. 39 (above left). This mask is unusual because of the strength of its carving, including eyelashes and tattoo marks, as well as the cigarette. Fig. 40 (above right). Caricature of a Spaniard about 15 in (38.1 cm) tall, produced near Mexico City. Fig. 41 (below). Aztec warrior, reading monk and campesino from other areas; the two small figures are from Guadalajara and the tall one (actually a candlestick) from Morelia.

Fig. 42 (above left). Lounging jaguar 8 in (20.3 cm) long, is a compound of a shaped branch of copal with tail and legs tacked on. It is orange with brown markings. Head is carved from the branch, but ears are tacked on. Fig. 43 (above right). Dog is carved from a bent branch, with legs, tail and ears added. It is from Oaxaca Fig. 44 (below left). Granadillo stylized bird and deer, each about 10 in (25.4 cm) high, from Guerrero. Fig. 45 (below right). Fantastic dragon assembled from whittled pieces in Yucatan is about 18 in (45.7 cm) long and ingeniously put together from pieces of approximate shape.

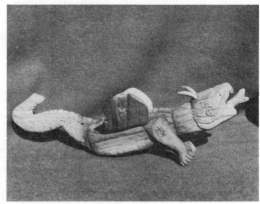

Fig. 46 (above left). Horse and lion in copal, from the Oaxaca area. Fig. 47 (above right). Rooster, hen and kitten, each about 3 in (7.6 cm), are whittled from a cedar-like wood and stained black. They are from Argentina. Fig. 48 (below left). Pony, bull and moose are from Argentina and are assemblies of shaped pieces. Fig. 49 (below right). From Peru comes this stylized bird. The design and wood are pre-historic, but the carving is modern.

CHAPTER VI

Simple Units; Unusual Result

Spanish Colonial furniture and a
Greek instrument share chip carving

When the Spanish came to the New World, they built towns and colonized at a much greater rate than they could import furniture and fittings from home. Besides, it was much less costly to have the Indians make what was needed. Thus, in northern Mexico, which then included the states of Arizona, New Mexico, part of Texas and California, there evolved a distinctive furniture design called Spanish Colonial. Individual pieces were utilitarian and tended to be blocky. They were usually of pine, which was plentiful, and stained dark to represent Spanish oak. They often incorporated elements of leather (chair backs and seats, table surfaces) which was tooled or braided, and wrought iron (braces, drawer pulls, handles, stretchers). Decoration consisted of very simple units, as shown in Fig. 50, plus chip carving and occasional designs of Indian origin. The effort was to produce something serviceable, long-wearing and comfortable.

Fifty years or more ago, furniture manufacturers produced a series of designs supposedly based on the Spanish Colonial, called "Mission," but as usual with quantity manufacture they were overdone and clumsy. Mission furniture had a brief vogue, then became the epitome of "Grand Rapids furniture"—and passed very far out of style. In recent years, there has been a revival of interest in the Spanish Colonial style, particularly in the Southwest, because the furniture can be made without a lot of frills and special shaping, and the decoration can be done with relatively few tools and skill. Above all, the furniture is comfortable. It is well worth trying.

Chip carving—making designs by cutting out triangular or square wedges with a knife—need not be dull and a mere space filler; it can be the major decorative element and has been used as such by people all over the world. The lyra sketched in Fig. 51 is an unusually fine example of the application of chip carving.

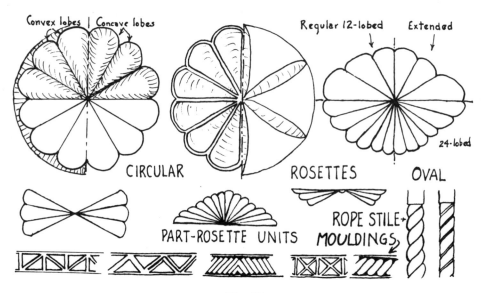

CIRCULAR ROSETTES OVAL

PART-ROSETTE UNITS

ROPE STILE→
MOULDINGS↗

Fig. 50.

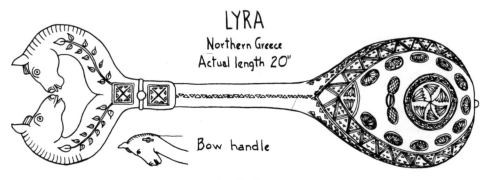

LYRA
Northern Greece
Actual length 20"

Bow handle

Fig. 51. Lyra.

CHAPTER VII

Have Fun with Holly
or
Other Dense Wood

Designs for small pieces

Thin slabs of holly or other distinctive and dense wood can be formed into a wide variety of interesting pieces. My interest in this specialty came about through seeing and copying the small angels and children whittled by Ruth Hawkins of Brasstown, North Carolina. Her figures are made primarily as Christmas tree ornaments, and I found that a number of designs could be readily adapted both for this purpose and for pendants, mobiles, awards, flat decorations and mounted silhouettes. I have made as additional designs such diverse pieces as an angel with a trumpet, a little girl rocking her doll and various flowers, all small enough to be worn as pendants. I have also made silhouette mobiles like a ballet-dancer group and a page with a sword. Pieces set on individual bases, such as a female swan with a cygnet, ducklings and a kneeling camel are all double-sided so they can be posed at will.

Another possibility is the assembly of several levels or planes, typified here by the old-fashioned racing driver with his goggles. The front of the car radiator and outlines of the front tires are whittled separately and mounted on the front of a walnut base block. The radiator ornament, for contrast, is a flying bird, in the round, glued to a top projection on the radiator. About an inch behind this element is a second panel, consisting ᴐf half a steering wheel with two gloved hands gripping it. And another inch or so back is the silhouette of the upper body of the driver. All these elements are detailed with low-relief incised lines, but the driver's goggles are given extra emphasis by being separate discs of holly glued in place. The assembly is quite realistic and three-dimensional when viewed from the front.

A closer "sandwich" of elements is typified by the gnome-house interior. This is based on a trick used by German ivory carvers on extremely elaborate miniature scenes, such as a series of deer feeding in a forest. The scene is actually made up of several layers carved separately, then laminated together to look as though they are a single high-relief pierced piece. In my case, I used four levels, all but the back one $\frac{3}{16}$ in (4.8 mm) thick. The front level includes a waving gnome and some tree forms. The next level is actually two smaller pieces, one of a female gnome and the other of a child playing with a pet mouse. The third level carries a low-relief depiction of the far wall of the house, showing a kitchen stove, a door, and two pierced openings, one for a bathroom, the other for a bed-cupboard. A fourth layer, about $\frac{3}{8}$ in (9.5 mm) thick, is hollowed out to show the interior of the bathroom with the "throne" and the bed in the cupboard.

Because the original shapes were cut from a small bush trunk, the two largest pieces have an interesting top curve and some black lines caused by branching. I decided to retain these—in fact, they dictated the design. The top of the composition looks like the top of a hill, and panels one and three are spaced apart to let light in on the two pieces of panel two and the low-relief carving of panel three.

The final major piece is a seven-unit mobile of ballet dancers in varied poses and costumes. Basic support arms are 4 in (10.2 cm) long, of fine piano wire retaining the curve of the coil. Units are suspended by mono-filament nylon glued into holes. (Knot the end of the cord before putting it in the hole, or it will slip in the glue.) This mobile, probably more than any of the other pieces, shows the possibilities for detail with holly. Although figures are 4 in (10.2 cm) tall at most, it is possible to depict finger positions, which are so important in ballet, and to detail faces and garments. (If you are using a less dense wood, simply increase the size of elements, to perhaps double those I used.)

Figures are all whittled from blanks sawed with a fine-bladed scroll or fretsaw, and the saw is used as well for such delicate work as separating fingers. Finished figures are not sanded, but are sprayed with a crystal finish or clear varnish to preserve the light color. To increase gloss, they can be polished with wax or natural shoe polish.

Panel #1

Panel #3

Panel #4
(Hollowed)

Panel #2 Units

4-PANEL ASSEMBLY (All panels ³⁄₁₆" except #4 = ½")

GIRL & DOLL

"Bold"

DUCKLINGS

"Shy"

Can be robed or not as desired

SWAN & CYGNET

ANGEL W/ TRUMPET

BALLET DANCER

Radiator ornament

Goggles

Nose

Steering wheel can be set in holes in base

Tire (2)

Two-hump Camel - Resting

Speed Maniac - 3 panels

Fig. 52. Pieces that can be whittled from holly.

Fig. 53. This ballet mobile consists of seven figures, individually carved on both sides from ⅛-in (3.2-mm) holly. Tallest figures are under 4 in (10.2 cm). Poses were taken from news pictures and reduced to a common size. Figures can have stylized faces, if this is a problem, because they are so small. Scale is not vital—note the man tossing the girl.

Fig. 54. This elaborate sandwich includes four 3/16-in (4.8-mm) layers. Major panels are 4 in (10.2 cm) long and piece-carved. They have the original shape of the holly piece on top, to help the suggestion of a cave. Lady and child gnomes are carved from scraps and serve as spacers to admit light between first and third panels. Fourth panel, a scrap to provide interiors to toilet room and bedroom, is ¼ in (6.4 mm) thick for needed depth.

Fig. 55. Christmas tree decorations can be ⅛-in (3.2-mm) holly, carved on one side. These are about 4 in (10.2 cm).

Fig. 56 (left). This camel was an addition to a holly Nativity scene. Available wood was not large enough to carve a standing camel, so this lying-down posture was substituted. The walnut base prevents tipping. Overall length is about 2½ in (6.4 cm). Fig. 57 (right). Three ducklings and a swan are also based to avoid tipping. Height of each is about 1½ in (3.8 cm).

Fig. 58 (above left). These pendants range from a 1-in (2.5-cm) circle for the rose to 4 in (10.2 cm) height for the page with sword. Roses have been antiqued by applying a darker stain and wiping off immediately, to leave cut areas darker. Fig. 59 (above right). These two 4-in (10.2-cm) beaver caricatures on skates, male with hockey stick and female with bouquet and bow, were awards for the coaches of two juvenile skating teams. Skates are integral and differ in design. The backgrounds are matching walnut plaques ½ in (12.7 mm) thick, with incised lettering filled with white pigment and varnish. Fig. 60 (below). Olympic aspirant show mementos were 1¼ × 1¾ × 3/16-in (31.8 × 44.4 × 4.8-mm) pendants for the girls, paperweights for the boys. The beaver on skates, in relief, is a caricature. He is juggling the five Olympic rings, incised in the background.

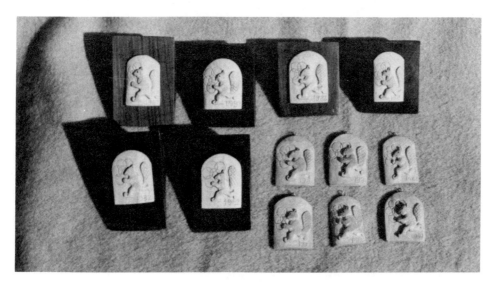

 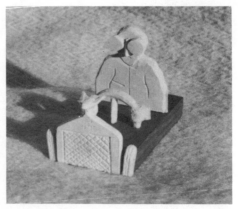

Fig. 61 (above left). A ⅛ × 2½-in (3.2 × 63.4-mm) holly figure and kite are assembled on a walnut base, with a "kite string" of music wire connecting them. Holly is good for such miniatures. Fig. 62 (above right). A spaced sandwich mounted on walnut depicts a racing driver. Tires and radiator are mounted on the front of the block, and the radiator has a three-dimensional bird as a cap ornament, as well as the carver's signature for a nameplate below it. Two gloved hands grip a section of steering wheel for the center element. The driver is a simple silhouette, except for the addition of a nose and two goggle lenses for accent. Fig. 63 (below left). Holly can be used as a substitute for ivory. Here is a playful walrus pup 2½ in (6.4 cm) long, in holly (left), with the original of Alaskan walrus ivory (right). Eyes and flipper tips are accented with black ink. Fig. 64 (below right). This 1¼-in (3.81-cm) tree frog pendant has ebony bulging eyes. Again, the density of ivory makes carving of the toes easy.

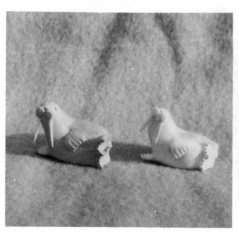 

Ebony insert

FROG PENDANT

44

CHAPTER VIII

Rustic and Realistic Figures

Wade Martin carved what
he saw around him—and well

Most of the carvings I see at shows or for sale in shops are at least some-what familiar in design and execution; a high percentage in fact are copies of familiar predecessors. It is, therefore, always a thrill to encounter carvings with really original subject matter or execution. These few pieces by Wade Martin are cases in point. I discovered them in the Brasstown, North Carolina, home of a retired couple who formerly ran a shop and kept a few choice pieces. My inquiries since then have uncovered only the fact that Wade Martin lives in the vicinity of Asheville, North Carolina, and is still alive, although so aged that he is no longer carving. These pieces, however, have a freshness, originality and true-to-life quality about them that I wish I could attain. They can be an inspiration to any carver.

The pieces are of a soft wood, probably pine, and finished without color. One is a self-portrait, and all show close observation of remote mountain people of the Southern Highlands. Scale is not constant; the blacksmith is somewhat smaller than the other figures, and the dogs are variously sized. I have included from the same collection a mirror frame in walnut done by an uncle of the present owner about 100 years ago. It is unusual in that the foliage design is limited modestly to two sides of the frame.

Figs. 65–67. Fig. 65 (above left). Boy with gun and pup is said to be a self-portrait of Wade Martin, and the country fiddler a portrait of his father. Each is about 8 in (20.3 cm) tall. Fig. 66 (above right). The woman with children is said to be Wade's mother, and the seated whittler a self-portrait. The latter is one piece—no separate stool. Fig. 67 (below). Blacksmith and anvil are to smaller scale, here distorted because the anvil was closer to the camera. The moonshiner with gun and jug is a familiar mountain subject of past years.

MOONSHINER

46

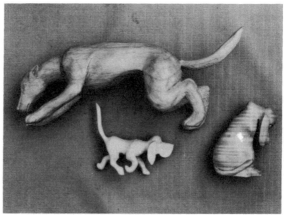

Fig. 68. Hounds are somewhat familiar, but the poses are alive —even the very dejected 2-in (5.1-cm) pup, carved cross grain in a strongly grained wood.

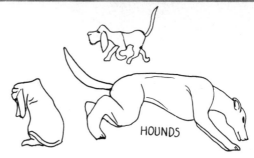

HOUNDS

Fig. 69. This mirror frame of walnut is unusually restrained, having foliage only on two sides. The design is apparently from a swamp oak or something similar. The usual treatment of frames crowds in foliage in an overly ornate pattern.

Fig. 70. In contrast to the thin and rough-finished hounds is this jackrabbit, fat and sleek. He is about 4 in (10.2 cm) long, in pecan.

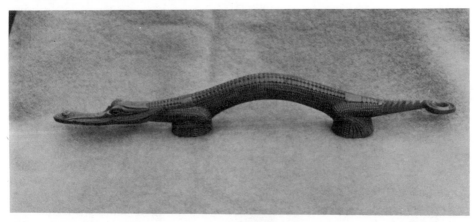

SPECIAL NOTE: Though this stylized crocodile door handle from the Sepik River, Papua New Guinea can be made with a knife or chisel, it is easier when chisels are used. (Chiselling techniques are discussed on the next page.) Crocodile is 1½ × 2½ × 16 in (3.8 × 6.4 × 40.6 cm), in a light wood, and has texturing. Legs are cross-hatched, back of oval scales, and tail is notched. Eyes are inserted, and could be carved, of course.

CHAPTER IX

Chisels Add Versatility

Variety serves special needs
and aids in faster cutting

Whittling—carving with a pocketknife or another single tool—is rather distinctly American, probably stemming from isolated pioneer ancestors who carried knives and used wood for a wide variety of purposes. In the countries of Europe, and indeed over most of the world, the chisel is a much more common woodcarving tool, whether it be the conventional chisel or the adz, which is really a combination of chisel and hammer or mallet. Strangely enough, the adz is the principal tool in the woodcarving countries of Africa, in Italy, in New Guinea and among the tribes of the North American Northwest Coast, but it is very uncommon among other countries of Europe, or in the United States. It is particularly suited to interior or concave carving as in bowls, dugouts and the like and has the virtue that it is a one-handed tool, leaving the other hand free to hold the work—and sometimes to get in the way.

Americans have taken up woodcarving as an avocation or hobby, and have gone at it as they have at other hobbies—putting a goodly part of their energies into trying to change the traditional procedure. As a result, there are some new forms of chisels (but far fewer than new forms of whittling knives!), and, of course, power has been added. Thus we have chain-saw carvers, pneumatic- or electrical-chisel carvers, rotary-tool (really a hand grinder) carvers, among others. Some of these methods reduce the rather boring time involved in roughing out a carving (which is a sort of paradox because the usual hobby is undertaken to fill otherwise idle time), and power tools are somewhat more dangerous than simple chisels. They may also generate noise or dust which can cause health problems, and they are not as versatile or as satisfactory as the hand chisels.

Woodcarving chisels have been made for some hundreds of years, so there is a language of sorts associated with them and with woodcarving itself.

Woodcarving chisels tend to be smaller and lighter than carpenter's or turner's chisels and available in a much wider variety of shapes. These make it possible for the user to carve forms and into places unreachable with a knife or other conventional tools—for example, a relief with a deeply sunken background or a relatively larger in-the-round figure, or the tiny details of eye and nose on a miniature. There are also available many auxiliary tools, such as riffler files, scrapers, routers, special saws and stamps. Selection of tools and auxiliaries is a function of the object being carved; it is not necessary to start out with a full kit of expensive tools. A very few will do very well for starters.

But first, this matter of language: The flat carver's chisel is sharpened from both sides, somewhat as a knife is, and is called a *firmer*, in contrast to the heavier carpenter's flat chisel, which is sharpened from one side only. The double sharpening makes it possible for the tool to be used on either side, and reduces the tendency for it to dig in or cut out. A firmer with the cutting edge at an angle instead of square across is called a *skew*. The gouges are made in a variety of *sweeps* or curvatures from almost flat to U-shaped. A small half-round gouge is called a *veiner* (it is used for carving veins in leaves), and a U-shaped one a *fluter* (it makes grooves that are called flutes). It is possible to get veiners and fluters as small as $\frac{1}{32}$ in (.8 mm) across. Gouges with considerable sweep are called *scroll* or *quick* gouges. Wider tools may be narrowed towards the *tang* (which is a point going into the handle); they are called *fish-tail* or *spade* tools. They are also lighter and better in close quarters. The body of the tool may also be bent in various ways so that the edge can reach difficult areas. Thus, a gouge may be *long-bent*, *short-bent*, *back-bent* or *knuckle* (see Fig. 71). It may also have a double bend, making it a *dog-leg*.

The woodcarver also has available the *V-tool* or *parting tool* (probably a carry-over from wood turning) which is V-shaped, thus having two cutting edges. The V may have an included angle of 30 to 90 degrees and is ideal for cleaning out corners, but is difficult to keep properly sharpened. There are also three-sided tools, which cut a flat-bottomed trench. If the sides are at right angles, the tool is a *macaroni*; if the sides slope outwards, it is called a *fluteroni*; with a back bend it becomes a *backeroni*. There is no need for those in your kit.

When chisels are used on hard woods and to remove large chips, they may be driven by a mallet. Any kind of club or hammer (soft-headed) can be used, but the traditional shape is like an old-fashioned potato masher. I use modern ones that have a plastic outside cover, in various weights—I find that a light mallet gives me better control of the chisel in detail carving than does an arm push, because arthritis makes arm muscles less than reliable. The soft-faced mallet also reduces noise and arm shock.

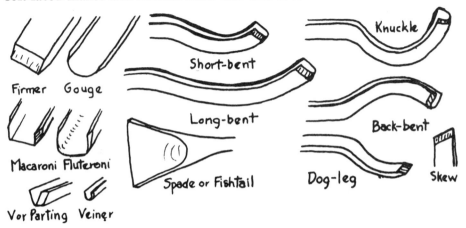

Fig. 71. Chisel shapes.

If you begin to feel that using chisels is more complicated than using the knife, you are right. And the end is not yet. With a knife, you can whittle almost anywhere, but with chisels it is safer to work at a bench or table large enough to hold both work and tools, unless you go in for tool racks. Also, the bench should have a vise or stop boards to hold the work you plan to do. Large panels usually do not require anchoring, nor do large in-the-round sculptures, but smaller pieces must be held to withstand the tools. In-the-round pieces can be held in a vise, or by a carver's screw, which is simply a headless lag screw screwed into the base of the workpiece, then passed through a hole in the bench, or whatever, so a wing nut can be tightened on the bottom. (You can buy a carver's screw or make your own from a lag screw.) Panels can be held in a bench block (see Fig. 72b). It is, of course, possible to make a special carver's easel that is quite versatile (also sketched), but it takes up space which you may not have.

My auxiliary equipment includes a power router, a sabre saw and a ⅜-in (9.5-mm) electric drill with sanding disc. Friends have band saws on the infrequent occasions when I need one. (Whittlers of small pieces have constant need for one; I don't.)

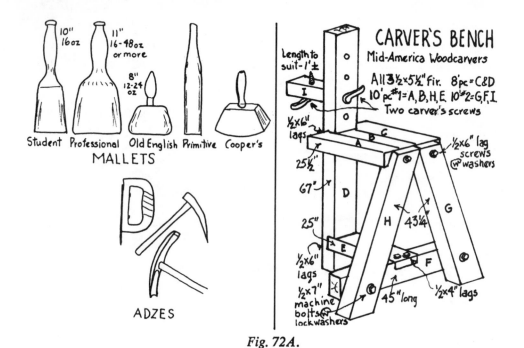

10"
16 oz
Student

11"
16-48 oz
or more
Professional

8"
12-24
oz
Old English

Primitive

Cooper's

MALLETS

ADZES

Length to
suit-1'±

½x6"
lags

25½"

67"

25"

½x6"
lags

½x7"
machine
bolts
lockwashers

CARVER'S BENCH
Mid-America Woodcarvers

All 3½x5½" Fir.   8 pc = C&D
10' pc #1= A, B, H, E. 10'#2=G, F, I.
Two carver's screws

A B C

I

D

E

H 43¼ G

F

½x6" lag
screws
w washers

45" long

½x4" lags

Fig. 72A.

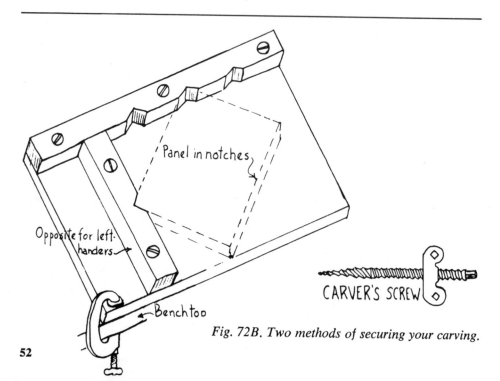

Panel in notches

Opposite for left-
handers

Bench top

CARVER'S SCREW

Fig. 72B. Two methods of securing your carving.

Chisels nowadays may be classified in various ways; some makers have their own numbering systems—a simple one numbers gouges by the radius of the sweep in sixteenths of an inch. The English have the "London system" that designates arc or sweep radius. The firmer is No. 1, a skew firmer 2, a very flat gouge 3, on up to a U-shaped one, 11 or 12. Special tools have higher numbers.

Tools are also designated by width of the cutting edge, ranging from $\frac{1}{16}$ in (1.6 mm) to $\frac{3}{8}$ in (9.5 mm) in sixteenths, on up to 1 in (25 mm) in eighths, and in larger steps on up to the maximum, usually around 2½ in (63.5 mm) for flat gouges. European tools are sized in millimetres: 1, 2, 3, 4, 5, 6, 7, 8, 10, 12, 16, 20, 25, 30, 35, and so on (1 mm = 0.039 in). Most suppliers now show cross sections of tool ends with their designations, so you can choose easily. Incidentally, I use carpenter's chisels and gouges for heavy roughing—they are cheaper and sturdier, but heavier and clumsier as well.

You may have a choice of handle on the chisels. Usual ones are round or octagonal, tapering towards the cutting edge, the better ones with brass ferrules at the tang end to inhibit splitting. Round ones are usually maple, ash, beech or boxwood. The octagonal ones may be dogwood (preferred in Germany). Octagonal handles are less likely to turn in your hand or roll off a bench. There are now plastic handles also, but I prefer the octagonal wood ones with ferrules. (You can, incidentally, turn your own handles and use short sections of pipe for ferrules.) Some tools, particularly short ones, are available with palm-fitting handles, like an engraver's burin. I prefer the longer handle because it gives more clearance for the mallet and less chance for barked knuckles.

I customarily sit down when carving, unless the piece is quite large. Many carvers prefer to stand. Thus, the table or bench you use should be suited to your preference. If you do many panels, for example, a sloping bench may be helpful, with a horizontal shelf below for tools. I find that on any given carving, I am unlikely to use more than 11 or 12 tools, so I don't have an elaborate tool rack; I keep the tools packed in shallow drawer racks. It is essential to have good light—a fluorescent tube is better than a single bulb, for example—and adequate ventilation, particularly if you sand, saw, or use hand-power tools. (For the latter, you may want a dust collector, goggles and mask as well.)

Years ago, I recommended six tools for the beginner: $\frac{5}{8}$-in (15.9-mm) firmer, ½-in (12.7-mm) flat gouge (fishtail), ¼-in (6.4-mm) medium gouge, ⅜-in (9.5-mm) scroll gouge, ⅛-in (3.2-mm) quick gouge, and ¼-in (6.4-mm) V-tool. To these can be added a ½-in (12.7-mm) scroll, a ⅛-in (3.2-mm) veiner, ⅜-in (9.5-mm) fluter and ½-in (12.7-mm) V-tool. H. M. Sutter starts his students with five tools plus an all-purpose carver's knife: ⅜-in (9.5-mm) No. 3 straight gouge, ⅝-in (15.9-mm) No. 5 straight gouge (these two preferably fishtail), ⅜-in (9.5-mm) No. 9 straight gouge, ¹⁄₃₂-in (0.8-mm) No. 11 veiner, and ⅜-in (9.5-mm) No. 41 parting tool. Other instructors suggest other combinations, sometimes dependent upon the sort of thing they teach.

Obviously, there would be a difference in selection for in-the-round and for relief carving. My advice is to start with a small number of inexpensive tools and add others as you find them necessary; beware of expensive multi-tool "sets." You can also make tools from old files or other steel, for example. H. M. Sutter has recently developed a series of short-handled and thin tools to ease the process of setting-in. Lastly, if you encounter a particular shape often, get tools to cut it cleanly and easily.

How to use tools

Important cuts with the knife are made simply by clenching the hand, and the blade edge is parallel to the line of the arm and hand, so cuts are made across. However, with chisels, the edge is at right angles to the line of the arm and hand; cuts are made by pushing with arm, rather than hand, muscles. This means that there is greater difficulty in controlling the cut exactly until you become fairly skilled, particularly if the wood being cut has grain or other hard spots. Both hands are normally used to hold the tool, one supplying the push and steering, the other actually acting as a brake to keep the tool steady in the cut and prevent it from overrunning (see Fig. 73); the exception to this is the palm or short-handled tools, which are usually pushed by flexing the hand which rests on the work, so they make many short scalloping cuts. When the mallet is used, the hand holding the tool both steers and restrains.

For heavy cuts, it is easier to hold the heel of the pushing hand over the tool-handle end and grip the tool in the fist; for light, delicate cuts, the pushing hand can grip more lightly and the cut can be steered by the fingertips of the other hand. I often let an index finger of the pushing hand rest along the line of the handle, as shown in Fig. 73. Also, the holding hand can hold a gouge or V-tool sidewise against a concave surface, also shown. Note that

I have *not* used the words "left" and "right"; you should train yourself to be able to shift hand functions—it is much easier than resetting the work or walking around the bench to work right-handed.

These suggestions apply both to in-the-round and relief carving, although in-the-round usually permits freer use of the tools—there is less likely to be wood vital to the carving beyond the immediate cut because the surfaces are usually convex. However, one of the first things to learn is how and when to make a stop cut. This is simply cutting *across* the grain before you cut *with* the grain, ensuring that the with-the-grain cut will meet the stop cut, thus preventing the wood from splitting out too far ahead of the chisel. Step 1 must always precede Step 2.

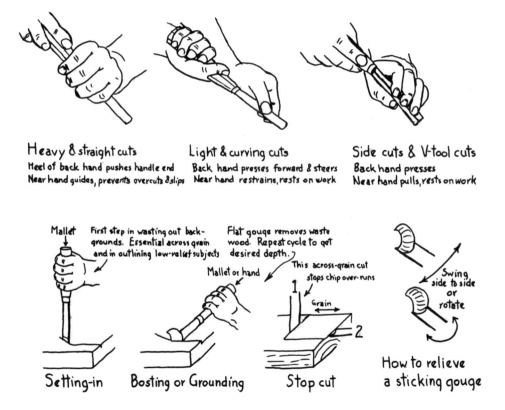

Heavy & straight cuts
Heel of back hand pushes handle end
Near hand guides, prevents overcuts & slips

Light & curving cuts
Back hand presses forward & steers
Near hand restrains, rests on work

Side cuts & V-tool cuts
Back hand presses
Near hand pulls, rests on work

Mallet
First step in wasting out backgrounds. Essential across grain and in outlining low-relief subjects

Flat gouge removes waste wood. Repeat cycle to get desired depth.

Mallet or hand

This across-grain cut stops chip over-runs

Grain

Swing side to side or rotate

Setting-in   Bosting or Grounding   Stop cut

How to relieve a sticking gouge

Fig. 73. How to handle chisels.

"Setting-in" is really an extended stop cut, and applies particularly to relief carving. This procedure makes it possible to cut away the background. After the design is drawn on a panel, the first step is to outline it with a small V-groove just outside the outer limits of the design all around. This cuts the surface fibres and provides a guide. Then appropriate firmers and gouges are driven vertically into the wood all along the V-groove to make an extended stop cut. This is usually easier with a mallet, and the chisel should be driven in only a short depth initially to avoid crushing the fibres on each side or starting an incipient split or breakout. About ⅛ in (3.2 mm) is safe in hard woods, double that in pine or basswood. When setting-in around a projection or other thin section be very careful—slope the chisel *away* from the section. The background is cut away up to the setting-in, and the procedure repeated until the desired depth of background is reached.

The usual tool for *bosting* or *grounding* (cutting away) the background is a relatively flat gouge, because it does not catch or stick at the corners as a firmer does. (Some carvers intentionally round the corners of the cutting edge on firmers to avoid this, but such a bullnosed tool cannot cut square and flat surfaces so well.) Gouges are also the primary tool for in-the-round roughing; the gouge cuts a trench and does not normally cause splitting at the edges, as a firmer may if in deep. The gouge is very versatile in such shaping—note Fig. 74 on how to relieve it on a heavy cut. The firmer is primarily a finishing tool, used to obtain a flat surface or a curved surface without tool marks and scallops. The rough shape of the subject is obtained with gouges; final *modelling* of convex surfaces is done with a firmer.

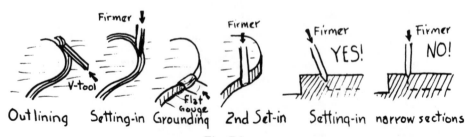

Fig. 74.

Particularly on backgrounds, it may be desirable to texture the surface—this breaks up impinging light and makes that surface look darker and more remote. There are many ways to texture, but I usually do it with a small fluter, cutting random scallops. The East Indian carvers almost uniformly use pattern stamps, which crush the surface into star or other patterns. Such stamps can be made of spikes by grinding off the points and filing on a star or other design, or leather-working stamps can be used. The same techniques can be used for texturing parts of a modelled carving—to suggest clothing, for example. Hair and beards and fur require more specific attention, and instructions have been provided in the chapters where such attention is needed.

In my opinion, it is easier and faster to use chisels than knives for most carving, although the knife is my favorite tool and I rely on it in a pinch. The skilled carver can accomplish miracles with sweep cuts—swinging free on any surface. It goes almost without saying that you should learn to watch the chisel cutting edge, not the handle top, when using a mallet, and that you should not try to cut off all the wood on the first pass. On cross-grain cutting, start at an edge and work in; do not work towards the edge or you will split it off. Keep your tools very sharp, particularly on soft woods, do not pry out chips or you will break the tool, and do not use chisels to open paint cans or strip insulation; that is what screwdrivers are for. Protect the edges, particularly when tools are stored.

CHAPTER X
This Totem Pole Lives

Articulated eyes, mouths and wings change position

The totem pole is not ancient; it is a relatively modern kind of carving, unique in that it was made only by Indians of the Northwest Coast. Early explorers of the Northwest Coast apparently saw none; the first mention is late in the 1700's. A Haida legend has it that the first totem poles were copies of one that floated ashore. This is quite possible because carved poles surprisingly like the earlier ones in America have been carved for centuries and put up to establish the boundaries of Korean villages—and net floats and other objects are carried from that area to the Northwest Coast by the Japan Current.

In any case, the Haida were the first American carvers of totem poles. They carved bountiful red cedar and adjacent tribes picked up the idea. As steel tools became available from white traders or other Indians in contact with white traders, the popularity of totem poles grew rapidly. From the early 1800's to about 1880 totem poles had a heyday. Now the only ones carved are for sale.

"Totem" is basically a household god or clan identification. The Northwest Coast was settled fairly recently; most of it was deforested by the last Ice Age. The Indians took as their totems the raven, the eagle, the black or brown bear (or grizzly bear), the beaver, the sea lion and the killer whale. Such totems had been carved on greenstone or argillite, and the totem pole was probably adapted from them. More recent arrivals in the area, like the deer, moose, porcupine, fox and lynx are not prominent on poles.

There were at least six types of totem poles. Originally they were house pillars or false pillars. Next came the mortuary pillar, which had at the top, or in a high recess, the ashes of the deceased. The memorial pole replaced it; it used symbols to recall a great man's deeds. Then came the heraldic portal pole—like a coat of arms among whites—and the potlatch pole, which celebrated a huge feast in which some individual or family had beggared themselves to entertain. Finally, there was the ridicule pole, which one household put up to deride or to call shame upon its neighbors. The height of the pole was determined by available cedars; designs were determined by the imagination of the carver.

In modern times, any number of vertical carvings have been loosely called totem poles. Most are not; they have no story or significance, merely a design. Some do not even have that, like some I made as a Boy Scout. The "totem pole" carved with a chain saw is not one—it is a modern adaptation. And the pole with relief carving on it is not a totem pole either—the totem pole is essentially one in-the-round animal atop another.

All this is a rather long introduction to the totem pole described here. But I felt that it was time for something different. So I made an articulated pole, based on the old designs, but modernized to the extent that portions move. There are three totems, all authentic—the eagle, the raven and the bear. However, all three can roll their eyes to show pupils, all three can open their mouths, and the eagle can raise his wings. For the fun of it, let us say that they can relax and rest between tourist pictures.

I used for a base the quarter of a basswood log about 17 in (43.2 cm) tall and about 4 in (10.2 cm) wide at the back. My plan was to include authentic designs taken from earlier totem poles and to finish them in color. To get the result I wanted, I obviously had to hollow out from the back and to add elements—but let us go through it on a step-by-step basis on the following pages.

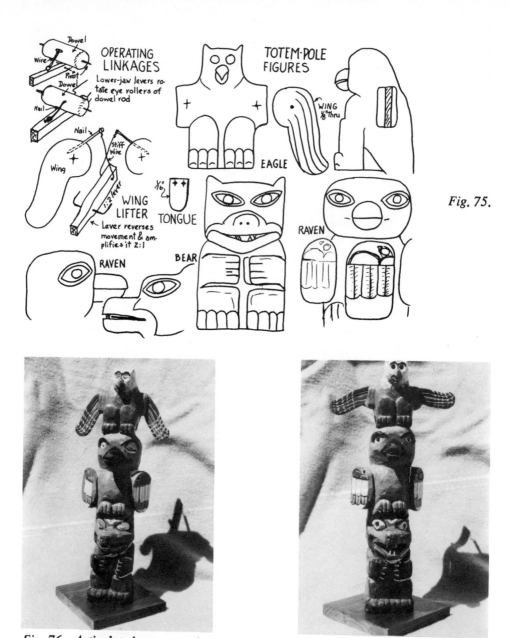

Fig. 75.

OPERATING LINKAGES

Dowel
Wire
Pivot Dowel
Nail
Nail
Lower-jaw levers rotate eye rollers of dowel rod

stiff Wire

Wing

1:2 lever

WING LIFTER

Lever reverses movement & amplifies it 2:1

TONGUE

TOTEM-POLE FIGURES

WING ⅛" thru

EAGLE

RAVEN

BEAR

RAVEN

Fig. 76. Articulated totem pole 17 in (43.2 cm) high and "sleeps" normally (left), but eagle's wings can lift and all eyes and mouths open when a back lever is moved (right). The miniature pole is basswood, a quarter of a log, painted with oils.

60

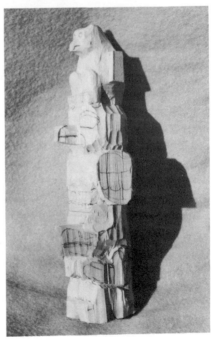

Figs. 77–79. Step 1 (above left). Block out the eagle with a saw. The core of the log is towards the front, thus providing a natural shape for beaks. Step 2 (above right). Eagle is blocked out with wing stubs instead of wings. Raven shape has been drawn below it —the eagle will stand on the raven's head. Step 3 (right). Raven and bear are largely shaped, eyes have been located and raven wings defined. This is done with chisels and mallet—it's faster.

Figs. 80-82. Step 4 (above left). Eye holes are drilled in, claws and mouths defined, and shaping mostly done. The holes meet in a slot in back—see Step 5. Step 5 (above right). A deep slot sawed and chiselled out in the back will accommodate the levers and operating bars as well as make it possible to hollow heads for the eye rollers shown with it here. Step 6 (right). Lower jaws are cut away and slots cut through to meet the ones in back. Also, slots are cut through the extended shoulders of the eagle so the wings can be fitted in.

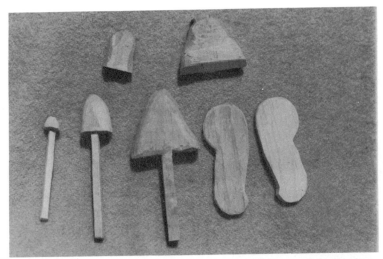

Fig. 83. Step 7. At top are the cutaway sections of lower jaws, which serve as patterns for their replacements, below, which have levers. Note wing shape.

Fig. 84. Step 8. Eye roller and jaw elements are fitted individually, with brads used as axles. Also, thin sections of wood are formed into tongues held loosely in the mouth roofs by tacks, so they will drop when the mouths open.

Fig. 85. Step 9. Now a vertical bar is set in place to tie the operating mechanism together. Levers may be pinned or wired to it—see Fig. 75, page 60.

Fig. 86. Step 10. Work with the motion to free it up and get maximum stroke, so eyes roll and mouths open as far as possible. When all is operating freely, saw off the axle brads (in a vise) and insert them securely flush with the surface. Mount the assembly on a stabilizing base—and you are ready for painting.

CHAPTER XI

The Brementown Musicians

Simple panel illustrates popular fairy story

Most children, here and abroad, have learned the story of the Brementown musicians, as related by the Brothers Grimm. It tells of four animals, turned out by their masters because they were old and useless, who meet in a forest. They see a lighted cottage, and by standing one atop another, find that it is occupied by robbers dividing their loot. The four "sound off" together, scaring the robbers away, then move in and live happily ever after. The story is commemorated by a bronze statue outside the town hall in Bremen, Germany.

I used a transparency taken some years back to project the silhouette directly on a walnut panel 1 × 12½ × 20 in (2.5 × 31.8 × 50.8 cm). Because the panel showed bark at the top corners, I rounded them off—the subject tapers anyway. The background was routed down ¼ in (6.4 mm), then smoothed and finished by texturing with a ³⁄₁₆-in (4.7-mm) radius gouge. The animals were modelled with knife, gouges and firmer. A coat of satin varnish sealed the surface, then walnut stain was applied to darken growth wood, with a second coat of dark walnut on the background to darken it more. Figures were sanded lightly to reduce the stain color, and the whole piece waxed and polished (front and back to reduce the likelihood of warping).

BREMENTOWN
MUSICIANS
Walnut Panel

Fig. 87

Fig. 88. Walnut plaque is 1 × 12½ ×
20 in (2.5 × 31.8 × 50.8 cm), with
rounded top to eliminate bark from
tree curvature. Design was projected
directly on the wood from a color
transparency.

Fig. 89. First step in carving is to rout the
background ¼ in (6.4 mm) deep, then
outline the design precisely by setting-in
with ⅛- and ¼-in (3.2- and 6.4-mm)
firmers and small gouges, grounding flat
with flat gouges, and sloping frame sides
up to a ½-in (12.7-mm) self-frame.

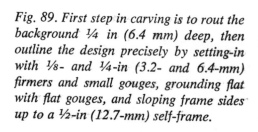

CHAPTER XII

Clouds-to-Sheep Metamorphosis

Step-by-step from pine blank
to relief panel with a smile

This panel in pine is relatively simple to carve and will help you learn to
handle firmers and gouges. The design is modified from a poster and provides
a smile as well as a carving. My blank was 2 × 12 × 14½ in (5.1 × 30.5
× 36.8 cm) and I laid out the composition directly on it. Now follow the
carving, step by step.

Fig. 90. Clouds become sheep in this pine panel,
2 × 12 × 14½ in (5.1 × 30.5 × 36.8 cm), painted
with oils.

Fig. 91. Step 1. Lay out the design to suit the available wood. I showed single sheep in various poses, some groups, and added a lamb or two as an afterthought. They are posed on a hillside, with clouds floating down so low that three are actually below the horizon; they repeat the general shape of sheep immediately below them. The original layout was in pencil; I tried not to overload the composition, and to vary poses. Shallow low-relief carving of the sheep has here been started as a test.

Fig. 92. Step 2. It may be advisable to alter poses of individual animals to improve the balance. In this closeup of the lower right-hand corner are two such changes, one lowering the head of the ewe at left towards the lying-down lamb, and the other to attain a more compact grouping at center, leaving a larger area of open grass. Legs must be sloped back towards the feet so they apparently are behind an irregular pattern of grass spears. Units have been outlined with soft-tip pen.

Fig. 93. Step 3. I decided to leave a border and slope in from it to the ground and sky. My testing indicated that a depth of only ⅛ in (3.2 mm) for the grass area was enough to set out the sheep, permitting the easy solution of setting the hill fold at left back an additional ⅛ in (3.2 mm) and making total depth of the grounding at the top ⅜ in (9.5 mm). This was worth the time of setup for routing, as was the ¼ in (6.4 mm). Note that routing is only approximate around the nebulous cloud shape, which is best determined as it is carved. Shapes are important only to avoid crowding and to suggest the transition to sheep at the bottom.

Fig. 94. Step 4. The remainder of the meadow is grounded out and left with vertically gouged scallop marks to suggest a grassy field. Clouds are carved in swooping billows, with very little undercutting. Individual sheep are modelled slightly, and pelt textured with irregular gouge scallops to suggest a fairly short coat of wool and avoid flatness which would reflect light. The grass is a tint of green, of course, darker in the distance, sky a light blue, and the sheep white with black eyes and slight antiquing with grey to bring out modelling. The general effect, however, is attained by not overdetailing the sheep.

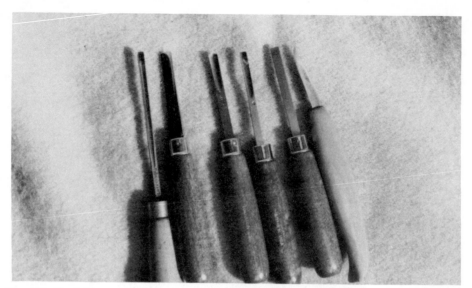

Fig. 95. Tool Note: Very few tools are required for cloud-sheep composition. Here are those I used (except for the router): left to right are a ¼-in (6.4-mm) V-tool; ½-in (12.7-mm) wide gouge, ½-in (12.7-mm) radius; ½-in (12.7-mm)-wide gouge, ⅜-in (9.5-mm) radius; ½-in (12.7-mm)-wide gouge, ¼-in (6.4-mm) radius; ⅜-in (9.5-mm)-wide gouge, and a whittling knife. The knife took care of details around the head, like the eyes and mouth, and was useful in general modelling. Even the clouds were left unsanded. Colors were oil pigments in varnish, and the finished job was given a spray coat of satin varnish to reduce the gloss. Then I made a sketch on paper for the record.

CHAPTER XIII
Silhouette Panels Are Easy

Six sports figures illustrate curling

Sports action figures are relatively easy to carve, and dozens of patterns are readily available in newspapers and magazines, often large enough to be traced directly. The figures can be carved either in relief against a panel, or as silhouettes such as these, which for some purposes are more effective because they can be displayed against a wall of contrasting color.

These six figures were harder to design because they depict curling, which is Canada's and Scotland's national sport and is played by many Americans as well, but rarely is pictured in the news. Actually, the earliest form of curling appears to have originated in Holland in the 1500's, but was developed and formalized by the Scots, who also established the international club and rules. The original rough-shaped boulders sliding down the ice have been replaced by very exact "rocks" with handles, made from a particular Scottish granite or whinstone. (Early Canadian players even used iron "rocks.") All the Scandinavian countries, Germany, Holland, France, Belgium and Switzerland have curling clubs, some operated by resort hotels. In the United States, golf and skating clubs are taking to the sport as a winter variation.

The four formal figures in this group were copied from a book on the sport and enlarged to an average height of about 6 in (15.2 cm). All are in ¾-in (19.7-mm) teak, to avoid possible warpage in the humid atmosphere of the club rink where they hang. The finish is a teak oil. The caricature of the tartaned Scot with his finger caught in the hole of an old-fashioned rock has brass tacks for jacket buttons.

Figures were sawed out on a band saw, then carved with relatively shallow relief. Maximum depth of carving is about ¼ in (6.4 mm), but much of it is less than that. The beaver symbol on the teapot refers to the particular club—the "teapot" does not hold tea, but Scotch, and is the portable equivalent of the 19th hole in golf.

BRUSHING START

Fig. 96. *This lady curler is in starting position, brush extended, left foot in the rack (starting slot). Note that she is left-handed. As she lifts the rock, she will swing it back and straighten her knee somewhat, then bend down and forward, as in bowling, when she swings it forward. This plaque, like all the others, is ¾-in (19.1-mm) teak.*

SKIP SIGNALS IN-TURN →

Fig. 97. *Curlers use brooms to sweep snow or loose ice chips away to maintain rock speed, or to brush them in front to slow the rock. The left figure is sweeping in front of a moving rock. The right figure is the skip signalling one of his three other curlers to slide his rock to the left of the visible standing one, with enough "English" so it will turn in behind it.*

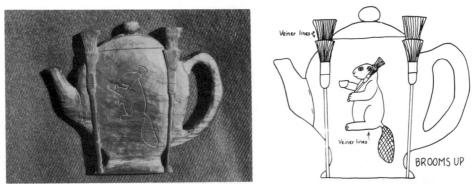

Fig. 98. "Brushes up" or "brooms up" is a curling term that means standing your brush upside down while you take a cup of "tea" to combat the cold. The broom is a special shape, with a very long and flexible double whisk.

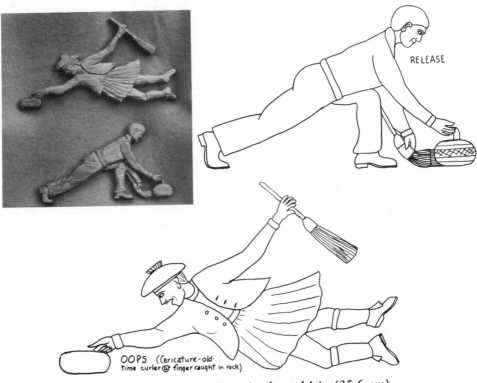

Fig. 99. Scotsman caricature is about 14 in (35.6 cm) long; the player releasing the rock is about 12 in (30.5 cm) long.

CHAPTER XIV

Remember the Point of View

Four small examples, including a cub, a whale and whaler, and skating beavers

Where will your carving be displayed? Will it be at eye level, above, or below? Will the light be good or diffused? It is obvious that the sculptured pediment of a building will be viewed usually from well below, and that any carving on a ship's stern will probably be viewed from above. But how about smaller carvings? I had one case. for example. of a fireboard—a closure for a fireplace in summer—that I tilted backwards at top so viewers could look at the carving without squatting.

Holly and walnut, the one very light, the other very dark, offer slight problems. It may be advisable to carve lines in them deeper than usual, to accentuate the shadows so the modelling is clear. It may also be advisable to texture some surfaces, to "antique" or darken backgrounds and grooving. It is not always possible to have ideal lighting or positioning—my living room tends to be dark and small carvings are high on a plate rail.

It is possible to vary the pose of a carving to enhance the viewing. The bear cub is an example. As a small carving, it can go anywhere, but as a larger one its logical position is on the floor, looking up at you. It makes an excellent doorstop, for example. Medium-sized carvings of dogs can be similarly posed. I have carved a number of animals, like birds and cats, specifically to go on shelves with their tails hanging down below their bodies and off the shelf, or looking over the edge—as some carvers designed eagles for cuckoo clocks.

The bear is from a 9-in (22.9-cm) cherry log, about 16 in (40.6 cm) tall. It was done freehand—no preliminary sawing of the blank. Most of the roughing was done with a 1-in (2.5-cm) carpenter's gouge, the finishing with woodcarver's gouges from a ⅛-in (3.2-mm) fluter for details like the eyes to a ¾-in (19.7-mm) medium-sweep one for the texturing. The surface was left with gouge marks showing, to suggest the rough fur of a bear cub, so the

Fig. 100. A 16-in (40.6-cm) bear, in cherry, designed to be displayed on the floor, looks up at the viewer appealingly. He is finished with tung oil, and is left with gouge marks, to suggest but not imitate the rough pelt, as well as to show hand carving.

Top of head

BEAR CUB

Fig. 101. A smaller version of the same pose, designed to be picked up, is smooth-finished, tinted, and has a wider stance because the wood permitted it. It is in pine, about 4 in (10.2 cm) tall.

Fig. 102. Bear head was fairly well delineated before the body was carved to get proper relationship between head and forepaws, as well as general pose. Carving was done freehand, without sketch or sawing.

gouge lines generally follow the direction of hair on the pelt. A V-tool was necessary for claw, mouth and nostril detailing. Holes were drilled between the legs, then the waste wood was cut out with a gouge. A slightly darker stain (walnut) on nose tip and eyeballs makes them stand out. Finish was with tung oil to get a low gloss.

This figure is essentially lifelike, but it is slightly caricatured—forelegs are lengthened and hind legs shortened for effect. In the hand-size version, the legs are more widely separated; the 16-in (40.6-cm) bear would have had to be several inches shorter to have the same stance because of log diameter.

Much more obviously a caricature is the award to "Superbeavers," a pair of beavers skating arm-in-arm. The two are about 5 in (12.7 cm) tall and one wears a short skirt—the award went to a couple long prominent in the Beaver Dam Club. Figures were whittled from walnut and wear aluminum skates set into a cross-section slab that suggests a pond. Lettering of the date, the names and the word "Superbeavers" was incised in the base and lightly tinted with white pigment in varnish. Prominent front teeth of the beavers were whittled from toothpicks and inserted. All of these details were necessary because the figure will probably always be viewed from close-up—in contrast to the bear cub.

Fig. 103. Twin beavers, skating, form an award which will always be seen from close up and at eye level, so details are important. Thus, the prominent teeth are whittled from toothpicks and inserted, the skates are thin aluminum, polished, and the cross-section-walnut irregular base has incised lettering whitened. Her skirt is lightly tinted blue.

A third example of viewing angle is provided by the whale and the sou'westered whaler—Moby Dick and Cap'n Ahab—which were commissioned for a table centerpiece. These also would be viewed close up and possibly in strong light. I chose to carve them of teak, each about 10 in

Fig. 104. Cap'n Ahab in process. He is teak, from a blank sawed in back and on both sides, about 10 in (25.4 cm) tall. Work to this stage is with chisels; details were added with a knife.

(25.4 cm) in its longest dimension, so the grain and pleasant color of the teak can be effective. The client specified that the captain was to have a telescope and a pipe, so I put one in each hand against the body to reduce the risk of breakage. Also, I provided Moby Dick with inlaid eyes of holly with ebony inserts, as well as with a double set of holly "choppers," and reared him up on his ventral fins so they would be definitely visible. The finish was tung oil again, for low gloss.

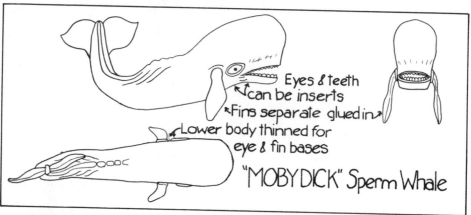

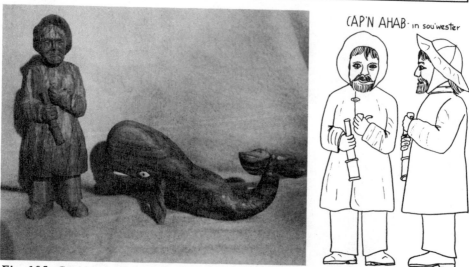

Fig. 105. Cap'n Ahab and Moby Dick as completed for a table centerpiece. Again, because of close viewing details are carefully worked out; the whale has inlaid eyes and teeth and "rears" on its ventral flippers, and the slight graining of the teak is enhanced by a low-gloss tung-oil finish.

CHAPTER XV
Derivative Poses

"Double silhouettes" fit available wood

The modern whittler and woodcarver differ from their earlier prototypes in that they work most often from milled lumber; the day of working from the log is largely over. Wood is expensive and good pieces are hard to find, but they usually have been kiln-dried, so the danger of checking and cracking during and after carving is greatly reduced. However, to obtain proper thicknesses of block for a particular carving may necessitate gluing up a blank or adapting the design to suit the available wood.

I find myself adapting with great frequency, and I have also learned to produce pieces with a reduced third dimension—not really in-the-round carving, but more nearly double-sided low-relief silhouettes. They look quite normal when viewed from front or back, but lack something when viewed from the side. However, a great many carvings nowadays are viewed only from one aspect because they are displayed against a background, so the silhouette is the primarily important element.

Several variations of one such design are shown in this chapter, all originating from one described in *Relief Woodcarving* (Sterling, 1982)—a girl studying a crystal ball. Two derivatives are a girl viewing a bird and a girl viewing herself in a mirror. Each introduces added problems and complexities. All were carved in rock maple because I had some pieces of it readily available. The girl with the ball is mainly a silhouette; the ball should be the center of interest, so she is an outline finished by gouge-scalloping. The girl with the bird is somewhat more defined, with two visible and separate hands, one holding a bird, so greater detail must be provided. The girl with the mirror combines medium relief and flat relief (in the mirror) and has stylized, textured hair, and well-defined hands and face. She is much more difficult than the girl with the bird, a major problem being how much modelling is required. I elected to do a medium amount, leaving visible flats on body and extended arm, for example.

One problem with a design such as this is that it must be "felt out" as you go on. To create the carving is an endless process of small decisions, each important in the way the carving will eventually turn out. The original drawing of this particular piece (on the wood) took only two tries. The first was too small in scale and inaccurate in proportion, so I turned the block over and drew a new and enlarged version on the other face.

The silhouette was band-sawed out. Then I found myself altering the outline of the face, the position of the shoulders and upper arms, even the relative location of the mirror and supporting hand. Part of the reason is that I had a third dimension in which to work; another part was that that third dimension was limited, so I had to foreshorten some elements. The arms could not be full thickness, nor could the face, nor the shoulders, so I had to modify positions of these elements so they "looked" right. I had to recreate the far side of the figure, locating the upper arm and shoulder so they made sense with the original view. Also, I had a forearm coming up to support the mirror, but there was, in the depth of wood, no place for the elbow, so it had to be assumed.

The mirror position had to be faked slightly because I wanted the image of the girl's face to be visible from one side. Fortunately, the forearm holding the mirror could be crossed over the other somewhat, thus supporting the partial forearm and positioning the mirror at mid-body more or less simultaneously. The mirror itself was at an angle, not a part of the face planes of the double relief that formed the body, so it required special treatment as well, and all this had to be allowed for as the blank itself was brought to general shape. The step-by-step pictures explain what I mean.

Fig. 106. The seeress, or girl with the crystal ball, is in 4-in (10.2-cm) maple (rear). Two derivatives are the girl with bird and the girl with mirror, each about 2½-in (6.4-cm) maple—because that was what was available.

Fig. 107. The girl with the bird involves separate hands, but also has an inadequate third dimension—the result of a choice between overall size and adequate thickness. She is finished with a scalloped surface.

Fig. 108 (left). The girl with mirror is more complex because the wood does not provide proper thickness for elbows and shoulders, necessitating compromises. These become more evident after the blank is sawed out and the right arm is defined. Fig. 109 (right). Mirror angle is important, as is relative position of the arms. Here the right arm is cut free and mirror position is in process of selection.

Fig. 110 (left). Further development thins the mirror and begins shaping the right arm and left hand, as well as the face. Fig. 111 (right). Features are defined and the hands shaped, as well as the neck and general contour of the head. Mirror position is determined as well.

Fig. 112. The left forearm will cross to a degree to make position logical. This view also indicated how all third dimensions are "cheated" somewhat.

Fig. 113. The wood is inadequate for the left elbow, so the left forearm must be anchored to the right arm, as shown here. Hair is textured with scallops.

Fig. 114. The completed piece suggests the reflection in the face of the mirror, but leaves the general silhouette stylized and somewhat blocky.

CHAPTER XVI
A Lettered Panel

An answer to the constant question: "What shall I make?"

"What shall I make?" is a question many amateur carvers, and sometimes professionals, ask. This is a case in point. A valued client phoned in desperation. Her son was in a dramatic production at his school, and the cast wanted to reward the three teachers who had helped with preparations for it. The play was "Godspell," which deals with the life of Christ according to St. Matthew. Only two days were available in which to produce the awards, and the budget was limited, so elaborate designs were out and religious motifs were considered inappropriate for the recipients.

My suggestion was that we award lettered plaques that could be hung or placed on a table as desired. I had incising in mind as being rapid and simple, but the client wanted raised lettering. I had some pieces of maple from which I could squeeze out three ¾ × 3 × 12-in (1.9 × 7.6 × 30.5-cm) blanks, so I designed a sort of scroll with 2-in (5.1-cm) block capital letters. This left room for a roll at the left but merely a curled edge at the right, particularly after a second telephone call that increased the number of panels to four and used the last suitable piece of maple.

I decided to make the letters ¼ in (6.4 mm) deep and to rout the backgrounds as much as possible. This was followed by setting-in around the letters with small chisels and levelling the background. The roll of the scroll at left and the curl at right were done by hand, as was texturing of the background with a small gouge cutting random scallops. (I use a plastic-headed light mallet for setting-in and much of this work; I can control the tools better this way than with the thrust of an arthritic shoulder.) The numerals '82 were placed one above the other in the space created by the final L, and the surface matte-varnished. Then walnut stain was brushed on and immediately wiped out, to create an antiquing effect—and we were done.

The plaques were a great success. In fact, the director of the show, another

Fig. 115. Three steps in carving plaques. Bottom, as routed. Middle, largely set-in (note tab end, which provides a clamping surface during routing). Top, as carved.

Fig. 116. Four plaques in maple, ¾ × 3 × 13 in (1.9 × 7.6 × 33.0 cm), after antiquing.

teacher who had been rewarded with a pair of tickets to a Broadway show, expressed regret that she had not gotten one. My client, who is very fast on her feet, explained that a special plaque was being made . . . then confessed to me what she had done. At the same time, she asked if I couldn't make another plaque as well as a remembrance for her son, who had starred in the production.

There was no maple of proper size, but I found a piece of cherry and one of oak, and made slightly more elaborate plaques, the one for the son including a star in the space created by the first L. Then the client had a further idea—could I make a small pendant with the word "Godspell" on it as well? The result was a holly carving with curved top and the word "Godspell" angled across it and "1982" incised in the upper right-hand corner. They were received with acclaim. End of commission.

Simple lettering can solve many problems. I would suggest, however, that it be done in a fairly hard and dense wood to reduce the problems of splitting. Incising letters with a V-tool is faster, but raised letters are more dramatic.

Fig. 117 (left). The emergency additions—at top, cherry and at bottom, oak. Fig. 118 (right). The final problem, a pendant in holly 1¼ × 1¾ in (3.2 × 4.4 cm), with raised ¼-in (6.4-mm) letters about 3/16-in (4.7-mm) high and incised date at upper right. Screweye is silver, with jump ring to match.

Fig. 119. Tools required include mallet (plastic-head cover), ½- and ¼-in (12.7- and 6.4-mm) firmers, two small gouges, V-tool (not shown) and special knife.

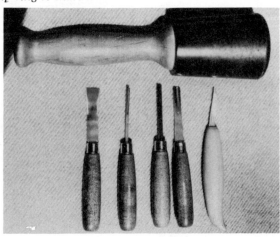

CHAPTER XVII

Carvings of Modern Japan

Simplicity and good finish are keynotes

There is still a very large woodcarving industry in Japan, although most of it is individual work rather than factory work, and the shops are mostly concentrated in tourist areas. Thus, I visited three one-man shops within a block on the holy island of Miyajima, and several shops almost side by side in Kamakura. (However, Kamakura was from 1185 to 1335 the effective political capital of Japan, with over a million people. Carvers came there from Kyoto to do the needed carving, and their descendants still carve—700 years later!)

The very complex pierced and painted panels that characterized old Japanese temples and shrines are no longer carved, apparently, and most of the pieces offered are very simple, with large areas uncarved. There is a tendency to concentrate on nature and the "old gods" (see next chapter). There are almost no caricature carvings in the sense of our current devotion to the hyper-ugly cowboy, Indian and sailor, but many of the carvings have a happy quality that ours seem to lack. They are, of course, the work of pros, and the traditional skill of Japanese carvers is very much in evidence. There are almost no painted pieces, almost no depictions of industry or urban life, no kidding of the olden times, nothing military.

Good carvings are as expensive in Japan, comparatively, as they are in the United States, so simplicity and the lack of carving over the entire surface may be influenced by economics. As would be expected, individual carvers specialize, and there is also specialization in areas. Thus, the beautifully carved plates come from Kamakura and Takamatsu, many figures from Miyajima, and so on. (Kamakura plates have a special lacquer made from poison sumach sap—which tends to limit the work force to those who are not allergic.) Incidentally, woodcarvings from all over Japan are sold in department stores in principal cities; the Japanese have little furniture by our standards, but many small *objets d'art*.

Certain woods are preferred for certain subjects, of course. Cryptomeria, something like our cedar and with alternating hard and soft strata like our redwood, is carved into animals, fish, dragons, etc., then apparently wire-brushed or sandblasted to make the winter-growth strata stand out. Boxwood is used for small pins and miniatures with considerable detail, and is given a high-gloss finish, so it looks like bamboo. A highly resinous pine is carved so that the figure is translucent and glows if a light is placed behind it. One carver I visited makes small turned boxes of various woods like maple, then carves the upper surface all over with a pattern of that tree's leaves. (Such boxes are expensive—around $50—but the same carver decorates a rice paddle with a scene including a torii or gate for a fifth of that price!) Some carvers specialize in *geta*—the wooden clogs Japansee women wear with the kimono. My wife has a pair in willow with a willow-branch pattern carved and tinted across the faces of the two geta (placed side by side).

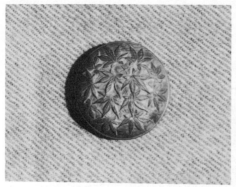

Fig. 120 (above). Japanese or scarlet maple provides the material and the design for this 2¾-in (7-cm) turned box, with all-over design on top. It is from Miyajime. Fig. 121 (right). Torii, or gate, against a minimalized scenic background adorns the face of this rice-serving paddle of a wood like our basswood. This carving is on a 4 × 5½ in (10.2 × 14.0 cm) surface, and overall height is about a foot (30.5 cm). The mountains and buildings are merely suggested, while the torii is detailed. No color or shading is used.

There are relatively few inexpensive toys or pendants in wood these days, principally because of the competition of plastics and metal. There is more carving in evidence now than there was a dozen years earlier when I was there, but the architectural uses are absent—not even store signs are carved. The old carvings are being carefully maintained, but there is no evidence of new ones on buildings.

I was particularly impressed by the few lines a carver used to achieve a recognizable design like a bamboo, willow or flower on the surface of a plate, tray, spoon or ladle intended for use. The effect is often obtained without deep incising and with little or no color contrast, so that the usefulness of the object is not impaired. On larger trays, the carving may be tinted and even be partially gold-leafed. On small pieces like spoons, the shaped piece may be stained, *then* carved so the base color of the wood contrasts with the stain. Finish varies widely, from nothing to flat stain or lacquer on small objects to elaborate traditional lacquering on plates. A spoon for dry tea will be stained only; one for wet tea and such a piece as a butter server will be elaborately lacquered. Usual objects are sanded prior to finishing, but the better (and more costly) ones retain the tool marks.

The Japanese carver uses chisels rather than the knife, as European carvers do, but his chisels are quite different from ours. They have short blades and long oval handles and are handled almost like pencils. They have thin, flexible blades, are tempered quite hard (*no* wedging out of chips), and are used largely without the mallet. Their saws and auxiliary tools are also quite different—saws, for example, tend to cut on the pull stroke, or in both directions.

Fig. 122. This textured tray with two gingko leaves is the famous red-lacquered kind from Kamakura. It can be cleaned with a damp cloth, and withstands moisture. It is one of many designs.

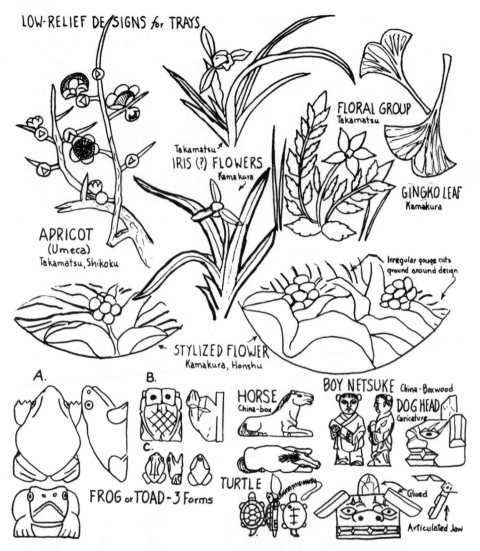

LOW-RELIEF DESIGNS for TRAYS

FLORAL GROUP
Takamatsu

Takamatsu
IRIS (?) FLOWERS
Kamakura

GINGKO LEAF
Kamakura

APRICOT
(Umeca)
Takamatsu, Shikoku

Irregular gouge cuts
ground around design

← STYLIZED FLOWER
Kamakura, Honshu

A.

B.

C.

FROG or TOAD - 3 Forms

HORSE
China-box

BOY NETSUKE China-Boxwood

DOG HEAD
Caricature

TURTLE

Glued

Articulated Jaw

Fig. 123. Low-relief designs for trays. Amphibians are a favorite gift between Japanese families, wishing long life and good luck.

90

Figs. 124–126. These three trays suggest the variety of forms and treatments in woodenware. All three are from Takamatsu and are sanded smooth to show the fairly prominent grain. The circular tray (above left) has an iris tinted with real gold, the floral group on the square tray (above right) is untinted, and the rectangular apricot tray (below) has faint tinting of the design. All are finished in clear lacquer, without stain.

Fig. 127. The short-handled tea scoops, used to put loose tea into pots, may be stained and carved afterward or simply clear-lacquered. The lion-head spoon at left and the larger tea scoop at right have no finish, while the tea scoop and butter spreader at bottom are red-lacquered in the traditional way.

Fig. 128 (left). These pendants include a 2½-in (6.4-cm) disc of a stylized thistle (tinted), another with a pert girl face and flower, the third an excellent stylization of a Samurai bust (double-sided) with separately carved legs hinged inside the "waist," and a small hammer suggesting the lucky god, Daikoku. Fig. 129 (right). The frog and turtle are significant to the Japanese, the horse to the Chinese. Here are small, lucky pieces, the frog and turtle at left only about ½ in (12.7 mm) long, thonged for attachment, plus a stained cryptomeria frog at top and a blocky one on its own base below. The boxwood horse is about 2 in (5.1 cm) long, and is Chinese.

Fig. 130. These silhouette pins of 3/16-in (4.8-mm) boxwood are deeply carved and finished in clear lacquer with a shine. They are relatively inexpensive and quite modern in styling.

Fig. 131. The Japanese also carve horn. That at left is water-buffalo horn with cranes, and pine symbols of long life. White and green pigments are rubbed into the scrimshawed grooves to make them stand out. The more elaborate cow horn from Okinawa is pierce-sawed at the top and decorated with a scrim-shawed temple scene filled with gilt.

CHAPTER XVIII
Ye Gods!—in Japanese

Popular carvings of the old gods provide a smile as well

It is customary for us to think of religion as a very serious matter, and to depict religious objects with restraint and almost severity. It is interesting, therefore, to look at some of the present-day religious carvings from Japan. That country has many religions, although Buddhism and Shintoism are the dominant ones. The old Buddhist temples and Shinto shrines are filled with magnificent and involved carvings, usually painted and pierced panels except for figures of the gods themselves. But modern religious carving is ultra-simple, almost plain, and unpainted; much of it approaches caricature. There is no austere, threatening element in it; it is friendly and happy. Also, many carvings perpetuate the symbols of which Japanese are so fond: the crane (national symbol of Japan) which represents long life, as do the toad (or frog) and the turtle. The badger and the frog bring good luck.

Many of the designs have been simplified over the years, like the Buddha and Fukurokuju figures; others retain traditional detail, like the Daikoku. The seven lucky gods vary somewhat from carving to carving, but the beards and implements, the build and pose, remain essentially the same, as they do in our depictions of saints. The distinctions are made from the accoutrements because the actual features are unknown. Undoubtedly, some of the simplification is a result of economic pressures. Carvings in Japan are relatively at least as expensive as they are in the United States, and per capita income is lower, so carvings must be simple to keep the price down.

Carvings shown here are current in Japan and amplify the preceding. They are amusing and friendly, if you want to try them. I have told as much as I know about each in the captions.

THE SEVEN
HAPPY GODS

Figs. 132–133. The seven lucky gods as a group on shipboard, each with his or her identifying symbols. This 6 × 13 × 15½ in (15.2 × 33.0 × 39.4 cm) carving was made from a wood like white pine, finished in clear lacquer. Deities, from left to right, are: Fukurokuju, bearded and carrying a stick, symbol of longevity; Benzaiten, the only female, playing a lute, symbol of music and culture; Bishomonten, long-bearded, in armor, usually carrying a halberd (not shown here), symbol of dignity; Jurojin, with long white beard (often actually whitened in carvings), carrying a golden jewel, symbol of popularity; Daikoku, carrying magic mallet and white sack, symbol of prosperity; Ebisu, carrying sea bream and fishing pole, god of fisheries and industry; Hotei, fat, carrying a stick and a big sack, symbol of a happy life.

Fig. 134 (left). Daikoku, the most popular of the seven, may be posed in various ways, but he carries an upraised magic hammer (reminiscent of the Norse Thor) and a white sack and stands or kneels on two sacks of rice. He is smiling and chubby. Here he is in white wood, unstained and unlacquered, 4 × 4 × 8½ in (10.2 × 10.2 × 21.6 cm), plus a 1¼ × 5 × 6-in (3.2 × 12.7 × 15.2-cm) base. Fig. 135 (right). Fukurokuju, associated with longevity, is stylized but caricatured as a stump figure with very high cranium (symbol of wisdom). He is about 6 in (15.2 cm) tall. The top of his stick is carved separately and inserted, and he is stained and varnished.

Fig. 136. Head of Buddha in white cedar is hollowed like a mask although it is only 3½ × 5½ in (3.9 × 14.0 cm). Note elongated, stylized earlobes, common on Japanese god figures, and the excellent treatment of Oriental eyes.

Fig. 137 (left). The traditional guard dog or lion at left is a Chinese carving, but I got it in Japan, where it is used as a temple guardian. This one is only 5 in (12.7 cm) tall, extremely detailed and elaborate in accordance with tradition. Beside it is an image of Daikoku, deity of prosperity, carved in the translucent resinous core of a pine bough, with the untouched wood swirling up from the base to back the figure. It has no finish—the resinous wood shines from the tools alone. Fig. 138 (right). Netsuke, the carved knobs that ended the thongs of a man's purse and were tucked through under the obi (sash) on the kimono, have become collector's items, so are being made both in Japan and China at a great rate. The little boy in back is a box-wood one from China, but the two in front are ivory and over 100 years old. That at left is the seven lucky gods in a ship with a chicken shape. The other is a scribe with bars for eyeballs, so they pop outward when he is tilted forward. The fourth figure is a Chinese lady in ivory, also an antique. She is tinted and her head is removable, connecting to a flat spoon for dipping the snuff she carries inside the Court.

CHAPTER XIX
Carve a Dragon

Five variations on a popular theme

Dragons, like unicorns, are a perennial favorite, but can be quite difficult to carve, depending upon their complexity. The legendary dragon, particularly the Chinese variety, has all sorts of excrescences around the head. It may have wavy tendrils around the mouth and/or ears, a spiky backbone line, hair or whatever on the backs of its legs, and some sort of addition to, or multiple forking of its tail. Because dragons are largely imaginary (except for the Komodo dragon), you can simplify the design somewhat to make it less fragile to carve, but in any case I would suggest a harder wood to repay the effort involved as well as to provide greater strength in thin sections. If you must have tendrils and elaborate poses, I would suggest carving your dragon as a relief panel; the background will then provide some support for fragile elements both during and after carving.

It is also possible to vary the backbone pattern and the foot pattern. Our general concept of a dragon is a lizardlike animal, so it would have clawed feet that can either be with three toes forward and one in back like a chicken or with four toes forward like a cat, although in both cases the toes should be long. The back ridge can be non-existent—in which case your dragon may look more like a dinosaur (as my caricature does); it can be a simple sine curve or a notched ridge (like my winged dragon); or it can have a wave pattern as the long dinosaur's back ridge does. Such decisions you must make because they are a function of what use you plan to make of the beast and how much time and skill you have. I have even seen dragons with back ridges consisting of spaced spikes carved from the solid! (If I undertook that one, I would carve the spikes separately and set them in drilled holes; they would be stronger and better, and so would my nerves.)

Here are five variations of the dragon theme, illustrating the preceding points. A classical Chinese dragon design is modified for relief carving on a walnut box top. Note the tendrils around the head and the multiple-forked tail. I also reduced the labor considerably by showing scales only along the back. This, too, makes the design less complex , as does the second, Fig. 140.

The third design is in pine, a stand-up dragon caricature modified from one carved hundreds of times by John Allan of Medford, Oregon. It has no back ridge and no scales.

Longest of the dragons is a 27-in (68.6-cm) snakelike pose in walnut, with undulating body and loop-the-loop tail. He also has no scales, but scales are suggested by the texturing, which is done by scalloping the body surface with a flat gouge. The effect is almost as good as scales, and takes less than half the time.

The final and most elaborate of my dragons is a winged variety, with looped tail and folded wings so he would fit the piece of walnut I had available. I have, incidentally, frequently compressed the third dimension of subjects to stay within the limitations of commercially available wood. The two latter in-the-round dragons, for example, are carved in 2¾-in (7-cm) wood—because that is what I had. Given thicker wood, the wings could be extended more, but would be fragile.

If I were to make this particular carving again, I would make the back ridge like that on the elongated dragon; its slightly greater elaboration would go well there. This dragon, 16 in (40.6 cm) long, took 33½ hours, of which 15 were spent carving scales (including the difficult areas under the body and in the tail loop), as compared with 21 hours spent for the elongated dragon, of which only 5 hours were scaling.

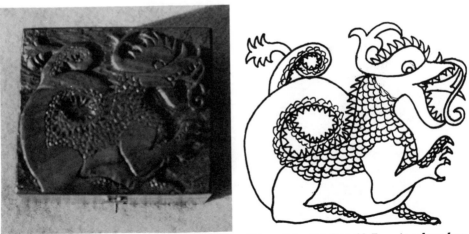

Fig. 139. Chinese dragon in low-relief on a 4¼ × 5-in (10.8 × 12.7-cm) walnut box top. Note elaborate tendrils about head, multi-front tail and tongue, partial scaling on back and foot tops.

Fig. 140 (left). Derived from a clay figure in an ancient Chinese tomb recently opened, this stylized dragon is very simple in design and a good project for the whittler or carver with moderate skill or time. The only detailing is in the head. A good size is 6 × 6 in (15.2 × 15.2 cm), from a 2-in (5.1-cm) blank. This carving is by Hugh C. Minton. Fig. 141 (right). Simple dragon, really a caricature, could be mistaken for a dinosaur. It is in pine, about 6 in (15.2 cm) high, and stained. Eyes and belly are shaved after staining to regain the base color.

Fig. 142. Completed sinuous dragon is 27 in (68.6 cm) long and about 5 in (12.7 cm) tall. It makes an excellent over-door decoration, and the texturing gives a realistic scale effect at that distance.

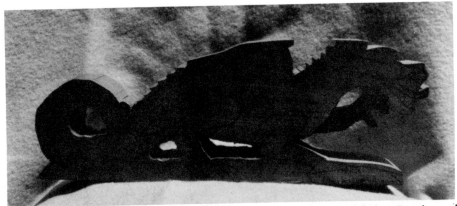

Fig. 143. The winged dragon requires a more complex blank. It can be bandsawed, but then must be drilled and shaped under the belly and the tail and inside the curve of the tail. Some of the complexity could be avoided by eliminating the integral base. It is walnut, 3 × 5 × 16 in (7.6 × 12.7 × 40.6 cm) long. If thicker wood were available, the wings could be spread more widely.

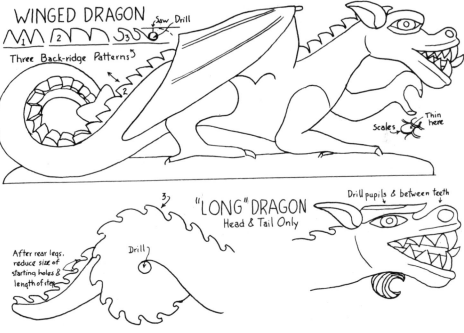

WINGED DRAGON

Saw Drill

Three Back-ridge Patterns

Thin here

Scales

"LONG" DRAGON
Head & Tail Only

Drill pupils & between teeth

Drill

After rear legs, reduce size of starting holes & length of steps

Fig. 144.

Whether or not your dragon has scales is a decision you will have to make based on the amount of effort you want to put into the carving. The answer, of course, lies in the areas difficult of access. It would be far easier to scale the long dragon despite his double-whirled tail. The winged dragon has an integral base, so it is difficult to reach his chest and belly, as well as the inner curve of his looped tail. The difficulty is, as always, that texturing must be done over all *visible* areas, and the eye can see where no tool will go.

The scale pattern of itself is simple. I create the rounded-end scales with half-round gouges of three sizes, $\frac{3}{16}$, $\frac{5}{16}$ and $\frac{3}{8}$ in (4.8, 7.9 and 9.5 mm), so scale size can be graduated down towards the tail and underbelly and on the upper legs. (Large fluters, which have a U-shaped cross section, would make longer scales faster, but I have none sufficiently large.) If the gouges are set in so the ends of one meet the tops of the two below it, the gouge itself completes the setting-in, but the scales will be very close and inflexible in pattern, so going around curves and the like will be complicated. I prefer to make the scales slightly longer, so the loops of one row stand away from the loops of the preceding one. This will often require use of a small V-tool to extend the ends of each scale until they meet the preceding loops. Once the stop cuts are made, the scales are shaped individually by shaving off the inner end of each, so the rounded ends of scales in the preceding row apparently stand above it. I do this with a $\frac{1}{8}$-in (3.2-mm) firmer so I can work around the loop, except where I cannot reach with it and I must use a knife. The knife and V-tool may be necessary to rough-shape scale outlines in such areas as the inner part of the top of the tail loop. (If the figure is carved without an integral base, there is more clearance for tools, but the piece is harder to hold while shaping and there is constant danger of breaking off legs.)

One problem with making a patterned texture such as scales is that extra scales must be added on the outside of a curve, if the added spacing between rows is excessive. This can be done easily by forking the scale pattern at the sides. This is easier to do than it is to describe. Another problem is presented by the necessity of bringing the scale pattern up to an edge, such as the ridged back; every other line of scales will require a half scale there. This can be handled by using a shorter gouge of the same radius if one is available, or by simulating the half curve with a V-tool—which is often easier and quicker.

The third problem is with grain on such surfaces as the looped tail; one must be constantly aware of the grain direction to avoid splitting off a scale during shaping of the base. The fourth problem is that any gouge tends to break out the wood inside during setting-in, particularly if the set-in is across grain. The problem is accentuated by driving in the gouge at a backwards angle, or even by driving it in straight. It is easier to bullnose the gouge cutting edge slightly (so the ends of the arc are slightly behind the center), then drive it in at a slight forward angle (with the handle ahead of the cutting edge). This relieves the stress on the entrapped wood.

When scales are cut, there may be tiny splinters here and there. Cut them off as you go, and clean up the job; they will be hard to find later.

Fig. 145. The selection of tools for carving the scaled, winged dragon includes a special knife, ¼- and ½-in (6.4- and 12.7-mm) firmers, gouges ranging from ¾ in (19.1 mm) flat to ¼-in fluter and long-bent half-round (to get scale pattern in otherwise inaccessible places) and V-tool. The longer dragon, because it is not scaled, goes much faster and requires fewer tools.

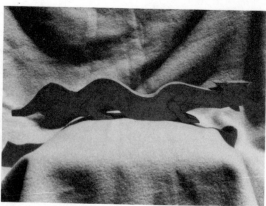

Fig. 146 (left). A comparison of heads and skin textures of the major dragons. Both are in walnut, the winged one somewhat more detailed in head and body. Fig. 147 (right). Both larger dragons were made from pieces of walnut plank about 2¾ in (7 cm) thick, so bandsawing of the blank made sense and saved time. The only complicated parts of the long dragon are the head and looped tail.

Fig. 148. Spines on the long-dragon backbone have a wavy shape, produced by drilling spaced small holes across the ridge as shown at left and sawing in to them, then cutting away one side in a long curve.

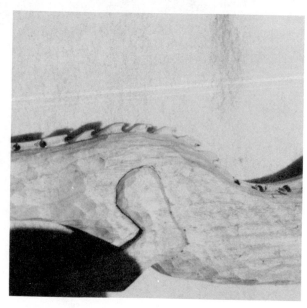

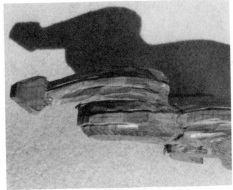

Fig. 149 (left). The mouth is formed by drilling between the teeth with a tongue visible between. The tongue could be extended at the front. Fig. 150 (right). The double loop of the tail can be confusing. I made it as simple as possible by showing the loops parallel on top and making the entire crossings underneath. The ridge is also carried down onto the tail-tip wedge ultimately.

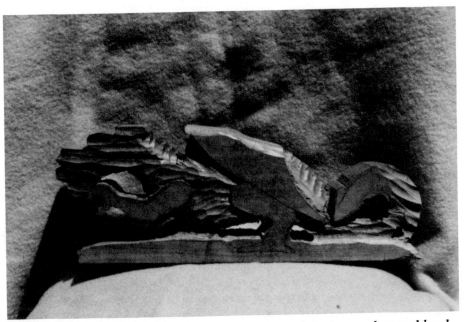

Fig. 151. A large gouge is the fastest way to clear off excess wood around head and tail, and will be useful as well in removing the wood on the far side of the upraised left foreleg. Don't forget the curvature of the tail!

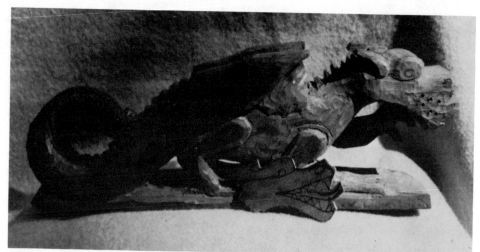

Fig. 152. Sawing is an alternative to gouging away wood around head and tail, and will be useful as well in removing the wood on the far side of the upraised left foreleg. Once again, don't forget the curvature of the tail!

Fig. 153. Graduated scaling done with three sizes of gouge covers the body, tail and upper legs. (This took two days!) Lower legs and toes are covered with cross-hatching rather than scales; it goes quite well with the more exact design elsewhere. Claws are delineated and long. Difficult areas to scale are the inside of the tail loop, under the belly and bottom of the tail, and the inside of the raised foreleg; they are visible but hard to reach with tools. Note that the wings are treated to look leathery, like bat wings.

CHAPTER XX
Ideas from the Trobriand Islands

Remote from white man influence,
these New Guinea pieces are unique

The Trobriand Islands lie perhaps 100 miles (160.9 km) north of the eastern tip of Papua New Guinea, and are part of that relatively new republic. They are visited infrequently by tourists because they are off the beaten track, so the natives have not been strongly influenced by the white man. They live as they always have, almost nude and in grass-thatched shacks, but they produce some of the finest and most original woodcarvings available. These are made without power equipment of any sort, and include circular bowls, long hollowed-out drums, and many small objects that we would start on a band saw. Also, the carvers usually work with very hard woods like ebony (black, macassar and striped), kwila (a light tan wood) and garamut (red-brown).

These people are Polynesian, not Melanesian—brown rather than black in color, but unlike other Polynesians, they use the adz extensively, particularly in rough-shaping such pieces as bowls and trays; they finish with chisels rather than knives. Also, a great deal of the decoration on flatter objects is incised designs that are unfamiliar to Western eyes—heavily stylized versions of ancestral designs drawn from prawns, fish and the like. They do show many whirls and curves, as do Maori designs.

The islands are quite small, so animal life is limited except for domestic imports like the dog and the cat. By our standards, surface decoration there might be considered ornate. It frequently incorporates inlays of nacre (mother-of-pearl), and occasionally of opercula like cat's eyes from other shellfish. Coconuts form a part of the diet, and coconut shells are used as carriers for such materials as the powdered lime taken when betel nut is chewed. So coconuts are decorated with a kind of scrimshaw—a pattern into which pigments may be rubbed.

The carving here is distinctly different from the more familiar work along the Sepik River in Papua New Guinea proper, which is more primitive and tends much more to the large, somewhat grotesque depiction of the human face (masks and shields) and utilizes a great deal of color.

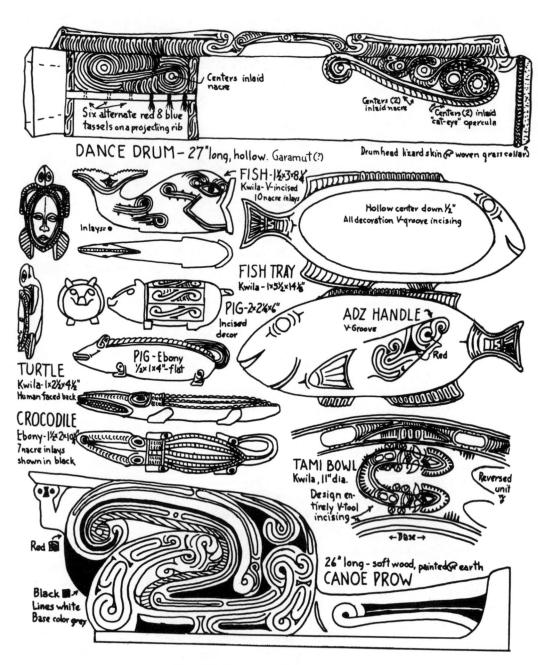

Centers inlaid
nacre

Centers (2)
inlaid nacre

Centers (2) inlaid
"cat-eye" opercula

Six alternate red & blue
tassels on a projecting rib

DANCE DRUM - 27"long, hollow. Garamut(?)

Drumhead lizard skin (or woven grass collar)

FISH-1½x3x8½
Kwila-V-incised
10 nacre inlays

Hollow center down ½"
All decoration V-groove incising

Inlays = ●

FISH TRAY
Kwila - 1x5½x14½"

PIG-2x2¼x6"
Incised
decor

ADZ HANDLE
V-Groove

Red

PIG - Ebony
½x1x4"-flat

TURTLE
Kwila-1x2½x4½"
Human faced back

CROCODILE
Ebony-1½x2x10½"
7 nacre inlays
shown in black

TAMI BOWL
Kwila, 11"dia.

Reversed
unit

Design en-
tirely V-tool
incising

←Base→

Red

26" long - soft wood, painted (in) earth

CANOE PROW

Black
Lines white
Base color grey

Fig. 154. Trobriand Island pieces.

Fig. 155. Bowl of kwila wood, 11 in (27.9 cm) in diameter by 3 in (7.6 cm) deep, from Tami Island, has an incised design that suggests a shrimp. It was adz-carved by eye, not on a lathe, and finished by rubbing the sanded surface with a boar's tooth. Color is tan.

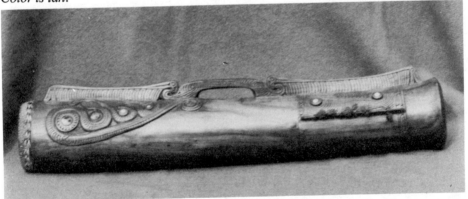

Fig. 156. Elaborate drum of garamut wood is 4 × 26½ in (10.2 × 67.3 cm), plus the projecting handle, which is integral. The drumhead is lizard skin edged by a braided grass collar. Handle and collar at right are patterns of incised lines, with varicolored tassels and inlaid nacre on the collar. The pattern near the head is a pair of snakes in low relief, surrounding circles, two with nacre inlays, the other two with cat-eye opercula inlays. The maker said the hardest job was boring the wood end to end.

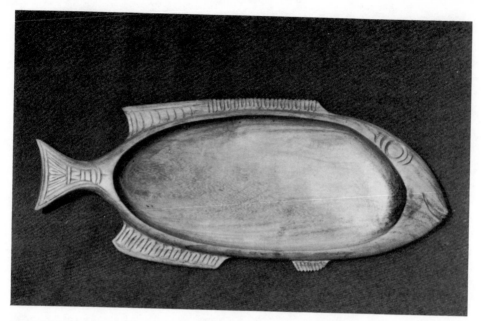

Figs. 157 (above) and 158 (below). Fish trays are a familiar product. These are of kwila wood, hence tannish, and finished with only boar-tooth rubbing.

110

Figs. 159 (above) and 160 (below). Seagoing canoes are quite large and fitted with outriggers and a woven reed sail. The formal ones have carved prows (above) backed by a double-eared shield. This prow is 1½ × 8 × 24 in (3.8 × 20.3 × 61.0 cm) and the shield (below) is about 2 ft (60.9 cm) square (it is not from the same canoe). Both have elaborate scroll carvings with pierced elements and are colored with earth colors of yellow and red, black from burned coconut, and white from lime.

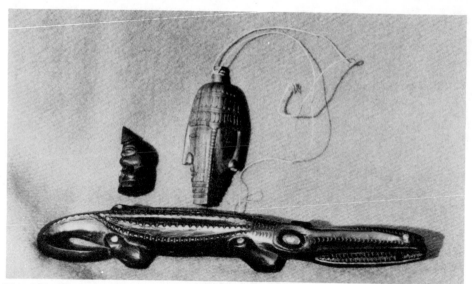

Fig. 161. Wood scraps are converted into an endless variety of small pieces. In this group, the little ebony idol at top left—about 1¼ in (3.1 cm) has a nacre-inlaid navel (see Fig. 164) and the crocodile below has nacre eyes and inlays. He is 10½ in (26.7 cm) long. The head above him is in a wood like walnut.

Fig. 162 (left). The two pigs, one circular in cross section, the other flat, are of ebony with scroll-carved decoration. The smaller is about 3½ in (8.9 cm) long. In Fig. 163 (right), are a stylized fish and turtle, the fish of kwila and the turtle of the walnut-like wood. The fish is about 1 in (2.54 cm) thick and 8½ in (21.6 cm) long and has four nacre inlays on a side.

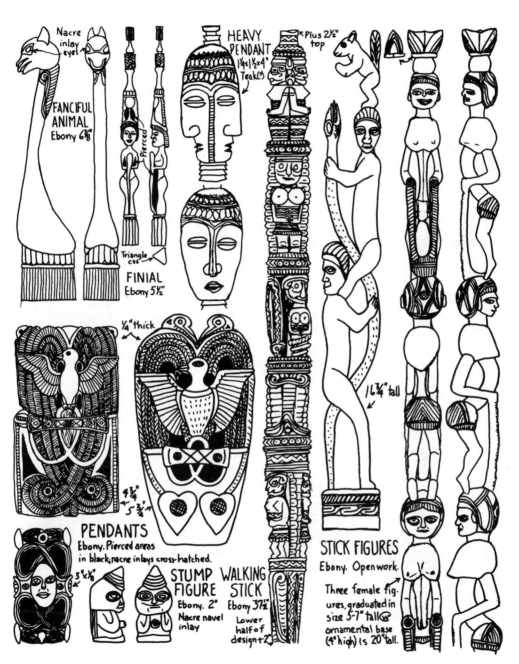

Nacre inlay eyes

FANCIFUL ANIMAL
Ebony 6⅛

Pierced

Triangle c.s.

FINIAL
Ebony 5½"

HEAVY PENDANT
1¼"x1½"x4" Teak(?)

Plus 2½" top

¼" thick

4¾"
5¾"

PENDANTS
Ebony. Pierced areas
in black; nacre inlays cross-hatched.

3½"x⅛"

STUMP FIGURE
Ebony. 2"
Nacre navel inlay

WALKING STICK
Ebony 37½"
Lower half of design +2"

1 L 3/4" tall

STICK FIGURES
Ebony. Openwork.

Three female figures, graduated in size 5-7" tall w/ ornamental base (4" high) is 20" tall.

Fig. 164.

113

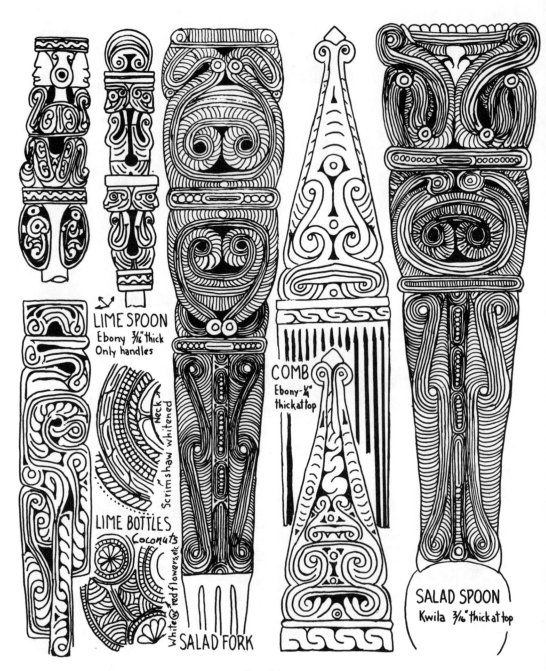

LIME SPOON
Ebony 3/16" thick
Only handles

Neck

Scrimshaw whitened

LIME BOTTLES
Coconuts

White & red flowers, etc.

SALAD FORK

COMB
Ebony - 1/4"
thick at top

SALAD SPOON
Kwila 3/16" thick at top

Fig. 165.

114

Fig. 166 (above left). The two statuettes are ebony, one-piece and 16½ and 20 in (42.0 and 50.8 cm) tall. That at left shows two men riding a snake, with a squirrel on top. The second shows three women graduated in height, stylized, each holding what may be a loop of cloth. There are nacre inlays where the hands meet the cloth.
Fig. 167 (above right). The walking stick at right is ebony, carved with a series of back-to-back mythical figures. The cane at left is from Palu, Celebes (Sulawesi) and is of macassar ebony, with a dragon's head.

Fig. 168. The two outer pendants, 2½ × 4½ in (6.4 × 11.4 cm) and 3½ × 5½ in (8.9 × 14.0 cm), are variations of the Papua New Guinea coat of arms showing the fish eagle and drum. Both have nacre inlays. The smaller center pendant has a head surrounded by tracery. All three are ebony and are under ⅛ in (3.2 mm) at the edges.

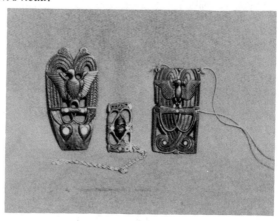

115

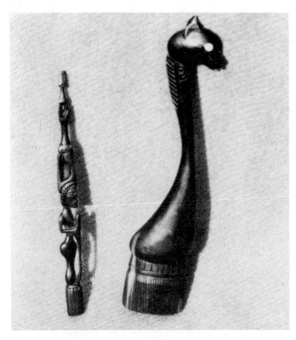

Fig. 169. Many small objects are made, usually from ebony scraps. These two are fanciful, that at left being a 5½-in (14.0-cm) female figure with elaborate headdress. It is triangular in cross-section, about ⅜ in (9.5 mm) on a side. The larger figure is a mythical animal with nacre-inlay eyes.

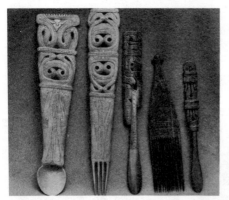

Fig. 170 (left). Intricate scrollwork with pierced portions is a familiar way to decorate flat surfaces. The salad set is in a light-colored but hard wood, the comb and the lime spatulas or spoons in ebony. Pieces range from 12 to 16 in (30.5 to 40.6 cm) and are 3/16 in (4.7 mm) thick at most. The lime spatulas and comb are used on the island; the salad set was made to sell to tourists. Fig. 171 (right). Coconut shells are made into lime carriers like the two end ones, or small baskets like the one in the middle. The end ones are scrimshawed and tinted, the middle one only incised.

Sharp Tools Are Vital

Traditional hand methods have been supplemented by machines

The necessity for keeping tools sharp turns off more embryo carvers than anything else. People don't like to take the time to sharpen tools, so they do not learn to do it properly, or they leave it until there are a number of tools to be sharpened. I can sympathize with all this because I hate sharpening, myself, and I do not do it well. The edge of a cutting tool is really a microscopic saw backed by two wedges, the first just behind the edge and the second extending back at the accepted included angle of 30 degrees, more or less. I say "more or less" because a thinner angle and sharper edge work better on softer woods, and a blunter angle is necessary to hold the edge when hard woods are cut or a mallet is used.

The objective is to reduce the number of microscopic feathery teeth and to reduce their length, then to keep them as nearly aligned as possible. This is done by a series of sharpening steps, particularly when sharpening is done by hand. The first step is the rough grinding of the edge to an approximate angle; this is usually done by the manufacturer on a production basis and need not be repeated by the user unless the tool is broken or badly nicked. In fact, it is inadvisable for the user to sharpen a tool on a conventional grinding wheel under any circumstances, because he is almost certain to burn the edge, thus removing the temper. If you must grind, have a water-cooled wheel, or wet and cool the tool at least twice as often as you think necessary.

There are three additional steps to sharpening, and these should be your primary concern. They are whetting, honing and stropping. The first two are really fine-grinding operations, but done on a flat stone by hand rather than on a wheel under power. Whetting is done on Washita, a yellowish or greyish natural stone; honing, on Arkansas, a white, very hard, uniform and fine-grained white stone, or their manufactured equivalents. Some makers now have the two on opposite sides of the same piece. Slips, the small shaped stones for honing the burr off the insides of gouges and V-tools, are also made of Arkansas, or should be—beware of the coarse reddish "slips" that are sometimes offered. In day-to-day carving, honing is a frequent operation, one that pros do subconsciously while planning the next cut; whetting is much less frequent unless the wood is very hard or abrasive.

The final operation is stropping—the same operation a barber does with a straight razor. Properly done, it is two operations (about three strokes each), one on rough leather with an oily surface containing a somewhat rough or other fine abrasive, the other on a smooth leather surface containing only a little oil. All the operations on stones are done by pushing the tool edge *towards* the abrasive as you would in cutting; stropping is done by pulling the edge backwards. This aligns the tiny feather edges on the blade.

Nowadays, most tools are sold ground and whetted and with a proper included angle, generally speaking. (It will be worthwhile for you to eventually experiment with an included angle, particularly if you get into carving very hard woods, bone, ivory and stone, as I do frequently.) Knives are ground so that the blade itself has the proper angle, firmers have an included angle of 30 degrees, 15 each side of center, and gouges have a straight interior and 30-degree bevel ground on the *outside*. (Beware of pattern-maker's chisels with the bevel on the inside—they tend to dig in and are very difficult to resharpen by hand.) All that you should have to do is a little honing and stropping.

Some carvers, by the way, swear by a hollow-ground edge, one that repeats the curvature of a small-diameter grinding wheel, the sort of edge that is exaggerated in a straight razor. They claim that this makes honing and whetting easier because the angle behind the cutting edge is less than it should be, reducing drag. It is also claimed to make the cutting edge stay sharp longer, which may be true on soft woods but I doubt it on hard ones; my experience is that it may make the edge turn or nick. I should point out, in all fairness, that these are matters of opinion, and "experts" differ.

I have tried to sketch the motions used in sharpening tools, both to maintain their edges and to keep from wearing hollows in the stones. (Many stones become channelled from excessive center wear and this may result in dullness in the center of the cutting edge on a firmer as well as rounding or "bullnosing" of the outer corners, which we will discuss a bit later.) Stones should be kept lubricated with thin machine oil, or even a 50:50 mixture of machine oil and kerosene. This coating should be wiped off and replaced when it turns grey and gummy from included metal particles. Periodically, also, natural stones should be washed with benzine or gasoline, or boiled in water containing a little soda. This lifts out soaked-in oil and grit. The manu-factured stones are different in structure, and can be cleaned just by warming them in an oven, then wiping them off; the heating causes the oil to exude and bring the grit with it.

To sharpen a knife, I use a rotary or figure-eight motion (A), (Fig. 172), bearing down a bit harder as the edge is moving forwards and lifting the handle a bit part of the time to be sure I touch up the tip, which usually dulls first. Unless the knife is very dull, a few swirls on the hone should do it, followed by stropping. (Some of the time, unless the wood is very soft, I even skip the strop.)

Sharpness can be tested by trying the edge on a fingernail or on paper—it should stick on the former and slice the latter when drawn across (B), and any variation in the sticking or cutting rate will show dull or nicked spots. Test tip sharpness on a piece of soft wood. Then the blade is drawn for a stroke or two over each side of the strop (O), which for knife-stropping is usually on two sides of a paddle. Watch how a barber turns the razor over heel-first at the end of a stroke—it saves a second or two.

Carving chisels are sharpened in much the same way, particularly the firmer (D). However, because the gouge edge is rounded, it must be rolled as it goes over the stone, so all parts of the edge are stoned uniformly. This is tricky. Some carvers do it by sliding the tool sidewise (E), others do it by a more difficult straight push along the stone, rotating the gouge as it moves forward. Too much roll will bullnose or round the corners; too little will leave them dull so they tear the wood. Dullness in an area may be seen as a line of light (F), a reflection from a flat surface, along the edge.

Because all sharpening is done from the outer side, a wire edge or burr forms on the inside; it can be felt with the fingernail. It must be removed by passing a slip through (G), adjusting the passes so the entire inner edge is covered. The same operation is done in stropping with a piece of folded leather (H). Some carvers believe in making a very small bevel on the inside as well (G), to relieve drag. The tool can be tested with a fingernail as with the knife or by trying it on a piece of soft wood.

Note the sketches in (E); the edge of a tool should be square, not hollow in the middle or rounded at the outside corners. This ensures cleaner cuts. However, some carvers prefer to ease the corners a little to reduce their tendency to catch along an inner angle. I don't; I like them square, unless I make a real rounded bullnose to use the firmer as a flat gouge. Note the corner-relief trick in Sketch I, Fig. 172—it may help.

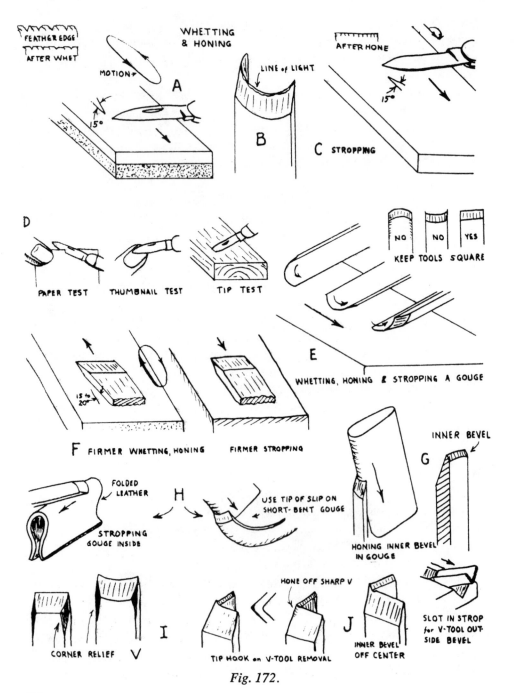

Fig. 172.

The parting or V-tool is a special problem in sharpening—which is why many neophyte carvers do not or cannot use it well. Inevitably, the lower point of the "V" will be slightly thicker than the side walls, both because of the shape itself and because a slight curvature will be left inside in manufacture. Thus, when the tool is sharpened, there is a tendency for a small tit to form at the V-bottom (J). Either one side or the other will have a small indentation near the bottom because of manufacturing inaccuracies or because you have been a bit too enthusiastic with a right-angle slip or stone on the inside. If the edge is square and sharp, as it should be, the tit can be removed by a bit of honing *outside* (J) as well as inside—and you will have one of the most versatile chisels in your kit.

All this is merely an outline of the intricacies of sharpening, but it should help to keep you from the habit of idle whacking or mistreatment of a tool while carving. It also helps to explain why so many carvers, hyperconscious of time as Americans are, have gone to mechanical sharpening, whetting and honing on sanding belts or buffing wheels, or even shaped wheels. There is danger that these methods will result in bullnosed tools, but many carvers do not mind slight radii at inner edges and on flat surfaces of carvings, although they do take away some of the crispness of the carving.

I will describe one such power-sharpening method in some detail—that of H. M. Sutter, Portland, Oregon, who is an expert on the subject. His equipment is relatively inexpensive and mostly homemade. (You can buy setups from several makers.) The first and primary machine is a belt grinder which takes a 1 × 42-in (2.5 × 106.7-cm) belt and is available from a number of companies, including Sears or Montgomery Ward. A series of backing blocks is added just above the table, the shape conforming to the sweep or curvature of the tool being ground. For rough grinding, Mr. Sutter uses a 60-grit belt. He finish-shapes with a 150-grit, and does final whetting with a 320-grit or crocus cloth. He feels that this produces a better and straighter edge than most people can obtain on handstones.

He produces the micro-bevel on the inside of gouges with a slip, by hand, and finishes it with a leather or plastic wheel and tin oxide. These wheels are mounted on a ball-bearing arbor mounted vertically and operated at 250–300 rpm. He has an assortment of wheels 6 in (15.2 cm) in diameter, with edges of various curvatures and V's to fit his tools. Some of the plastic discs are made very thin to fit inside small veiners and fluters, so they tend to bend. These are supported near their centers by thin plywood discs. Leather discs are made of old belting glued together and shaped with harness tools.

Wheels are coated with a very thin mixture of tin oxide in kerosene. An alternative is to mix the powder with water to which a few drops of detergent have been added. Another is to use the very fine abrasive used in polishing eyeglasses, or to use very fine rouge or some other abrasive oxide. Both sides of the cutting edge should be polished to a mirror finish—it reduces drag. The final operation is further polishing with a cloth-buffing wheel and tripoli wax. In normal carving of soft woods, the buffing operation will usually keep the tool sharp. Incidentally, a fine-grit 6-in (15.2-cm) wheel on this slow-speed mandrel will grind straight edges on firmers and V-tools without the danger of burning created by the typical high-speed modern grinder—it acts like an old-fashioned grindstone.

The necessity for resharpening and the danger of edge-nicking can be reduced by proper tool care. Keep tools on the bench or workplace side by side with their sharp edges towards you so you can select your next tool easily. Store them in slots so their sharpened edges touch nothing, and when you carry them, put them in a roll that covers but does not touch the ends. It is advisable to strop each tool after you have carried them in a roll—in fact, some pros strop each tool before they use it, as a barber does; a tool can lose feather-edge alignment just from sitting. Keeping tools from rusting goes without saying, but I will say it anyway.

Fig. 173. Commercial belt sander adapted to include a short arbor that will take a buffing wheel. It is, in effect, an extension of the belt-driving pulley.

Figss. 174 (above) and 175 (below). Leather and plastic wheels (above) are home-made and used on an arbor made by connecting an old washing-machine motor to a pulley-driven shaft, as shown below. Discs are shaped to fit the interiors of various gouges and the V-tool.

Some Finishing Suggestions

The first is "Use good taste and let the wood show"

Finishing is so much a matter of personal preference that I hesitate to make suggestions. I have mentioned, project by project through this book, how I finished my own pieces and, when I knew, how other carvers finished theirs. This, and general observation through the years, have led me to some general conclusions.

The typical cabinetmaker strives to attain a high gloss on his pieces by sanding in many steps and applying many coats of finish. So do some sculptors. But many professional woodcarvers try to achieve instead a soft glow, unless the carving is incorporated in a piece of furniture or there is some special reason for high gloss—like a carving of a supposedly wet seal.

With the rise of plastic and other copies, the tendency has been to avoid sanding to a high polish and to avoid using fillers; instead, some tool marks are left and the texture of the wood itself is preserved so the piece *looks* handmade. This is particularly true of the harder woods. For white pine and basswood, for example, the skilled carver applies thin tints of color to give variety without destroying the feeling of the wood. He does not apply a dark stain in the vain effort to make the wood look like what it is not.

My own method for soft wood without visible grain is to spray with matte or satin varnish to inhibit end-grain absorption of color. Then I apply tints and wipe them down immediately so the color remains in cut areas but is removed from higher surfaces and planes, thus suggesting the color but not denying the handwork or the wood. I use oil pigments in varnish, normal stains or ammonia-based stains, but acrylics can also be used. I also use colors or stains to get an "antique" or darkening effect in cut areas of any carving as well as to darken backgrounds, thus making the carving appear deeper than it is. Some of these stains include wax, and thus are really single-coat finishes, but I usually use either a good furniture wax or neutral Kiwi® shoe polish to provide final finish on interior pieces. For exterior ones, there are both gloss and satin varnishes that will weather quite well. The only problem is that they do tend to fill in the carved areas and will eventually almost obliterate the carving as well as make the surface look grey. My solution to that has been to use teak for outdoor pieces whenever possible—it can be maintained with semiannual coats of oil alone.

There are, of course, a host of special situations that require special finishing. Objects to be handled a great deal must be protected more than those which are not handled at all; this usually means varnish. Objects like bowls or ladles to be used with food should *not* be varnished. Some carvers use lacquers; I use a salad oil that will not turn rancid. Such carvings as coats of arms or basswood doors finished to resemble bronze require special finishing, such as gold leaf and antiquing; I have given detailed instructions for such specialized finishing in *Carving Religious Motifs in Wood* (Sterling, 1981). In recent years also, a great many "one-coat" or otherwise specialized finishes have been developed for woodcarving and cabinetmaking; these in general are designed for use after sanding and give too high a gloss for me. But many of my friends use them, particularly on small softwood objects made for sale.

How to Change Copy Size

If the drawing or photograph you want to copy is the wrong size, do not panic. A local graphic arts shop with a Photostat™ machine can copy it precisely to the desired size, or you can make a photo negative and project it (assuming that the original copy is too small, which is usual). If neither of these devices is available, there are several other methods.

The roughest is an elastic-band enlarger which will give you a rough outline for the silhouette, which may be good enough. (If one elastic band is too short for your purposes, link several together.) Anchor the band with a pin or thumbtack at one end and put a pencil in the other. Put an ink mark along the band to correspond with the desired enlargement: a third of the way for 3:1, halfway for 2:1, three-quarters for 1½:1, etc. As long as the band is stretched a bit and the ink mark follows the original outline, the pencil will sketch an enlargement, approximate, but often accurate enough.

If higher accuracy is necessary, you can make a pantograph, or buy one. To be useful, it should be made quite accurately. I have found it easier to transfer dimensions by one of two methods. The traditional one is the method of squares. Draw a grid of ⅛-in (3.2-mm) squares on transparent paper or plastic and keep it for use as needed. This is placed over the original photo or drawing. Now draw a grid of ¼-in (6.4-mm) squares on the board or another sheet of paper to double the size, ⅜-in (9.5-mm) squares for triple size, and so on. Copy the design square by square, as shown in the sketches.

I lose my place when using that system, and I have some competence at drawing, so I use the point-to-point method. I provide a base and side line on the original, either by drawing or by taping an L-shaped cardboard or paper square on it as sketched. Then I draw a similar square pair of lines on the wood or a sheet of paper. Prominent elements of the original are located on the copy by measuring their location with relation to the two faces of the square, and transferring these dimensions, multiplied by the desired enlargement, to the board or other copy. Thus, if an ear on an animal is 3 in (7.6 cm) up from the base and 2 in (5.1 cm) in from the side, and the copy is to be 1½ times the original, the dimensions are transferred as 4½ in (11.4 cm) up and 3 in (7.6 cm) in from the side. Locate as many such key points as you consider necessary, then sketch in the enlarged outline, as a child does in following the numbered dots in the comic pages. This method I find to be accurate and faster for me—simple arithmetic is my dish.

If the subject is large or animate and you want to make a reduced sketch, a series of photographs from the four points of the compass is helpful. Or you can make or procure proportioning dividers which sculptors use. These are simply double-ended dividers which can be set so that a dimension measured at one end will be reduced or enlarged by the desired percentage at the other.

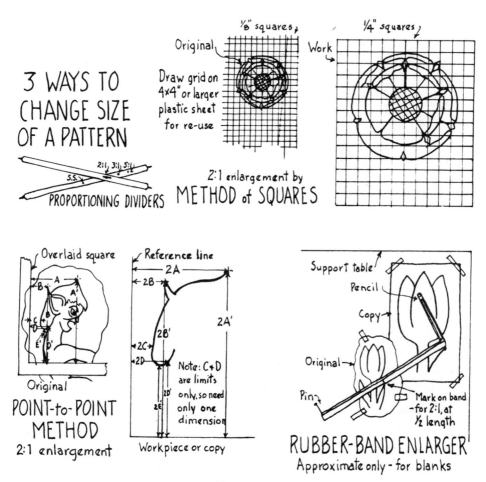

Fig. 176.

Index